EASY **DUTCH OVEN** COOKING

EASY DUTCH OVEN COOKING

Classic & Contemporary Recipes in 5 Steps or Less

Sara Furcini

Photography by Thomas J. Story

ROCKRIDGE
PRESS

Interior and Cover Designer: Jill Lee
Art Producer: Meg Baggott
Editor: Britt Bogan
Production Editor: Andrew Yackira

Photography © 2020 Thomas J. Story, food styling by John Belingheri

ISBN: Print 978-1-64739-697-8
eBook 978-1-64739-698-5

R0

TO
The Frayed Apron's
readers

CONTENTS

INTRODUCTION

My passion for cooking wasn't always apparent to me, but it was obvious to certain key people in my life. One of those people, my husband, unexpectedly gave me the gift of a class at a culinary school in New York City. Just one hour at the Natural Gourmet Institute was enough for me to discover my life's calling. To give you some idea, I'm pretty shy and never do anything like this: That same night, I practically sprang on the night manager, needing to know how I could, somehow, be part of the school. That's how I learned about a volunteer assistant program, and the next 4,000 hours of my future were instantly decided.

I first encountered a Dutch oven on my very first day as a chef's assistant. I'd seen these cooking vessels before, but I had never thought of them as anything special. Then, suddenly, Chef Jill called for a specific pot, "the orange one," and there I was lugging this 13-pound behemoth up from the depths of the storage rack, thinking, "What era is this even from?" The adzuki bean and squash stew with ginger juice she then began making is seared in my mind because of the absolute reverence she showed for the Dutch oven she used to cook it.

She just stood there stirring, and it was like watching a witch standing over a cauldron with something magical taking place in the room. The sage began her incantation, chanting how nice and hot the walls of the pot were, good for insulating the stew—the best pot for evenly cooking beans. Finally, she cast her spell, "This is the best pot in this kitchen. Everybody should own one," and my fate was sealed (especially after I tasted the stew!).

I immediately bought an affordable red Cuisinart Dutch oven. It didn't come with an instruction manual, but I thought, "Hey, I *am* in culinary school, so what the heck!" and started experimenting. I tested it on Boeuf Bourguignon (page 92), then Strawberry Rhubarb Crumble (page 161), bread rolls, potpies, chilis, bison stew . . . you get the idea. That pot became my best bud through culinary school. Eventually, I found myself reaching for it by default, and when I stopped to wonder why, I realized that everything coming out of it tasted better, cooked faster, and almost never failed.

Fast-forward to today: My Dutch oven is still my favorite tool, as readers of my blog, *The Frayed Apron*, know all too well. And what I can tell you after my years of experience and experimentation is that Dutch ovens are incredibly easy to use. I meet so many people who are intimidated by them that I decided to spread the magic. I hope you will join me and let me be your Chef Jill as you learn to love your forever pot, too!

HONEY GARLIC–GLAZED SHRIMP AND BROCCOLI, page 78

Get to Know Your Dutch Oven

CHAPTER ONE

Dutch ovens are incredibly easy to use, but it helps to know a little about when they originated, how they are made, and what they are used for. As you will see, they are so much more than basic pots. In this chapter, you'll learn about all the different shapes, sizes, weights, finishes, and materials these versatile cooking vessels come in, as well as which types of Dutch ovens work best for which types of recipes. Let's dig in and demystify this ancient tool so you, too, can begin cranking out delicious dishes in your home kitchen.

A Tool Built for Ease

There's a reason people swear by Dutch ovens. Whether you're an aficionado or just looking to try out that shiny new toy, a Dutch oven will transform your cooking life. Yes, most Dutch ovens are heavy, but they're incredible time savers. From stovetop cooking to oven baking, the modern Dutch oven is an all-in-one tool. It's so versatile that it can replace multiple pots, pans, and bakeware—and even aluminum foil. Dutch ovens also allow you to cook *and* store food for the week in one vessel, eliminating the need for multiple storage containers and simplifying meal planning.

Although their size and heft can be intimidating, Dutch ovens are durable, and many of the modern enamel-coated Dutch ovens are dishwasher friendly. Plus, the thick, metal construction that makes them so heavy is their best feature. It allows these pots to conduct and distribute heat efficiently so ingredients cook evenly and consistently, resulting in better tasting food that takes less time to make.

The recipes in this book are designed to help you put your Dutch oven to work every day. Everything you find here will be easy, straightforward, and no fuss: meals, sauces, and goodies that are a breeze to get on the table because they involve **no more than five steps from start to finish**. When you are really on the run, look for the recipes labeled 30-Minute Meal and One Pot. Whatever your schedule allows, your Dutch oven will soon become your mealtime hero.

HISTORY OF THE DUTCH OVEN

Many cultures around the world have a version of thick-walled metal cookware, but the term "Dutch oven" can be traced back to 1710, when the production process was refined using the Dutch method of casting relatively inexpensive iron in sand, allowing for a cheap alternative to brass. Thus began the mass production of this sacred pot.

The Dutch casting process allowed the vessels to have thicker walls and a smoother finish, expanding their usefulness and longevity. Over the last several centuries, the design has undergone many transformations, eventually evolving into proto-ovens for baking, stewing, and roasting.

Traditionally, Dutch ovens would be set over a bed of coals, or even covered with them, to create a hot internal cooking environment. You can still find examples of these earlier models today: Some cast-iron pots have legs for standing over coals; others have handles for hanging over open fire. Earlier pots often had rounded bottoms because they were better at distributing variable campfire heat over a larger surface area.

Most Dutch ovens today are enamel coated with flat bottoms. They still function like ovens, radiating and diffusing heat from a focused source around food. Though non-enameled Dutch ovens work perfectly well on the stovetop, the reverse is not true. You definitely wouldn't want to set your enameled pot onto hot coals or a campfire. Many people around the world still practice open-flame Dutch oven cooking, sometimes even as a competition. In fact, entire communities exist to uphold this cooking style, the largest being the International Dutch Oven Society.

There are no campfire recipes in this book (they're not exactly easy!). If you want to learn more about how to manage the variables of open-flame cooking, contact the International Dutch Oven Society or check out *The Frayed Apron* website.

The Most Versatile Cooking Vessel

Dutch ovens aren't just for stews. The benefits of evenly cooked food cannot be overstated, and Dutch ovens are so good at it that you can perform almost any type of cooking with them, with almost any heat source. Whether you want to attempt crème brûlée over coals, bread on a campfire, or ribs on an electric or gas stove, the Dutch oven's diffused radiant heat allows you to achieve nearly any texture you wish with your food. Furthermore, the pot's sturdy construction often allows you to perform multiple recipe steps using a single vessel—such as going from stovetop to oven. Let's look at the many ways you can use your Dutch oven.

Braising

Braising involves slowly cooking large pieces of food in a liquid (in the oven or on the stovetop) to ensure that they're moist and flavorful, and the Dutch oven can do this with even a small amount of liquid. The Dutch oven's high sides mean less water evaporates; the steam travels up, collects on the pot's sides, and settles back down around the food. Braising in a shallow pan requires more liquid (1 to 2 cups more if braising a roast in the oven). After braising, the cooking liquid can be simmered and thickened, or reduced, for a sauce. Boeuf Bourguignon (page 92) involves browning beef with onions and then braising them in red wine.

Roasting

Roasting employs hot, dry air to caramelize your food. Using your Dutch oven in the dry heat of the oven is a great way to encourage evaporation and concentrate flavors. For a convenient one-pot meal using this method, try Pork Tenderloin with Roasted Fennel (page 75), and don't forget to serve it with the pan drippings.

Stewing

Stewing is the Dutch oven's heart and soul, as this cooking method makes full use of your pot's volume. Similar to braising, stewing simmers bite-size food in water or stock. Many stews start with a foundation of onion, celery, and carrot (known as a mirepoix) or of onion, bell pepper, and celery (known as the trinity), with spices layered between vegetables, meat, and stock to achieve complex and dynamic flavors.

Sautéing

Sautéing refers to cooking food quickly in a small amount of fat, usually over high heat. This technique is often associated with fresh, 30-minute meals, such as stir-fries. Note that the Dutch oven's bottom may take time to warm up, but, once the pot is hot, you often don't need extreme temperatures. Be prepared to stir frequently and make sure to have all your vegetables prepped and ready to go to avoid bitter flavors and mushy food.

Baking

Baking involves surrounding batter or dough with hot, dry air in the oven. Many people use special cake pans, bread pans, and baking sheets when baking, but you can accomplish a lot in a Dutch oven with spectacular results. For example, your Dutch oven is especially suited for crunchy, crusty artisan-style bread! Bakeware is often made of aluminum, which is typically quite thin and cools rather quickly. However, a cast-iron Dutch oven is usually dense, making it better at conducting and retaining heat than aluminum pans are, meaning more carryover baking and shorter overall bake times. I usually remove cakes or breads from the oven 1 to 5 minutes sooner when using the Dutch oven because of this effect.

Frying

Frying is a great way to coax crispy textures from your Dutch oven. A pot with tall sides is perfect for frying safely and preventing splatters. There are two types of frying: pan-frying is done using enough oil to come halfway up the sides of the food (think bacon frying in its own grease), and deep-frying is done using enough hot oil (from 350°F to 375°F) to fully submerge the food so it can float (think French fries). The smoke point, or the temperature at which an oil begins to smoke, is very important to keep in mind, especially when deep frying. Thankfully, your Dutch oven will help you maintain an even temperature (and a thermometer can remove the guesswork).

Boiling and Poaching

Boiling and poaching are a lot like frying in that the food cooks in a hot liquid at a steady temperature. Water boils at 212°F, and the boiling method is ideal for quickly cooking foods such as pasta. On the other hand, poaching aims to cook foods gently in a flavored or acidic liquid just below simmering, from 160°F to 180°F. Red Wine–Poached Pears (page 154) is a classic poached dessert recipe. This cooking method is also great for pickling vegetables in acidulated warm water for a fun twist.

UNEXPECTED DUTCH OVEN TRICKS

The Dutch oven excels at more than just cooking.

→ **Use it for cold stuff.** Metal is great at distributing heat, but it's equally good at distributing coldness. This means you can use the Dutch oven to make ice cream cake or keep a salad cold by refrigerating the pot in advance.

→ **Weigh things down.** I can't tell you how many times I've used my pot to press water out of tofu, cook paninis in a skillet, or stretch pizza dough.

→ **Double up on cooking methods.** I love to set a steamer basket over roast meat inside my Dutch oven and quickly steam or wilt some fresh vegetables using the heat from the pot roast below.

→ **Transport food.** If you're bringing a dish to a potluck or party, there's no easier container for storing and reheating than a Dutch oven.

→ **Go from oven to table.** Keep dirty pots and dishes to a minimum during the holidays by using one vessel that is just as pretty on the table as it is functional in the oven or on the stovetop.

The Properties of the Pot

Dutch ovens come in a bevy of sizes, colors, weights, and shapes. Despite what you might think, the best ones do not necessarily cost the most; the best Dutch oven for you depends on how many people you cook for, how much storage space you have, and the kinds of dishes you like to make. If you already have the good fortune of owning one of these pots, understanding its characteristics will help you make better use of it.

Size

Most Dutch ovens are oval shaped, but some are circular or novelty shaped (such as a heart). They are all sized in quarts—the liquid volume they hold.

So, what's the right size for you? If you are cooking for yourself and another, a 4- to 5-quart pot should handle your needs. If you cook for a crowd or like to prepare larger cuts of meat such as pork shoulder or whole chicken, a 6- to 7-quart pot will ensure that food has space to cook evenly. If you have small burners or almost no storage space, consider a 2- to 4-quart Dutch oven, although you will sometimes need to alter recipes to achieve optimal results (see Modifying Recipes to Fit a Different Dutch Oven, page 8).

Beyond these considerations, your Dutch oven will, ideally, match the size of your burners, but it's okay if it doesn't. If your pot is smaller than the burner, be mindful of the fact that the metal sides will get hot and food may cook more quickly. If your pot is larger than the burner, the food may cook more slowly and less evenly because of the uneven heat dispersal. Stirring more frequently can help.

Weight and Material

Most modern Dutch ovens are made of several different metals, including cast iron, and many of these pots are enamel coated, which increases their durability. Enamel is typically dishwasher and oven safe and somewhat nonstick. Unlike earlier versions, enameled Dutch ovens don't require any seasoning (see Care and Cleaning, page 9).

The thickness of the pot's walls and bottom determines its effectiveness and weight. Heavier Dutch ovens take longer to heat but maintain temperature longer and diffuse heat more evenly than lighter models. A lighter-weight Dutch oven can be more convenient for recipes like soup and pasta, since it is easier to handle and pour from when it's filled to the brim.

There are high-quality stainless-steel Dutch ovens, too, but they are not usually enameled, and they heat foods slightly differently than their iron counterparts. I tend to relegate those to cooking lighter dishes, such as sauces or soups.

Brand

There's a wide range of Dutch oven price points, but I always say the best Dutch oven is the one you already own. I have a dorky number of Dutch ovens, and I regularly rotate among all of the different brands.

Le Creuset is probably the most iconic brand when it comes to Dutch ovens, and the brand is very well regarded by professionals and amateurs alike for consistency and quality. I cried when I was given a Le Creuset set, and I definitely notice they heat faster than my budget-friendly Dutch ovens—but we're talking about a difference of 60 seconds or so.

Lodge and Cuisinart make excellent pots that are a little more affordable and every bit as useful. These brands are in my collection and have withstood heavy use (really, I mean *heavy*).

I have found some budget-friendly off-brand gems as well, such as my AmazonBasics Dutch oven, but any pot will have its pros and cons. Your main consideration should be how durable the enamel is: If it chips on the cooking surface, the Dutch oven is, basically, ruined. For that reason, it's worth investing in a pot that has a warranty and a brand that has ironed out its quality control. Besides chipping, there are also heat maximums to consider. Some brands can be heated up to 500°F (Le Creuset), while others may only tolerate up to 400°F (AmazonBasics).

Here's a handy chart to help you choose the best Dutch oven for you.

DIAMETER (IN INCHES)	QUARTS	WEIGHT (IN POUNDS)	MATERIAL	SERVES
8	2	8	Cast iron	1 or 2
9¾	4½	9.6	Enameled cast iron	2 to 4
11	6	13	Cast iron	2 to 5
13½	6	13	Enameled cast iron	4 to 6
11½	7¼	12.8	Enameled cast iron	6 to 10

MODIFYING RECIPES TO FIT A DIFFERENT DUTCH OVEN

Every recipe in this book is intended for a mid-size (4- to 5-quart) enameled Dutch oven, but that doesn't mean you need to buy a new one if the one you have is a different size. With a few adjustments, you can make any recipe fit the pot you've got.

My pot is smaller.

→ With soups, stews, and stocks, use the same amount of solid ingredients, but use your pot to guide how much liquid (water, stock, etc.) you include; do not fill the pot beyond three-quarters full. When ready to serve, use a slotted spoon to portion the solids, add more liquid to the pot, allow it to heat, mix briefly, and then add the liquid to the solid servings.

→ With roasts, disassemble or chop the meat into pieces and use a thermometer to make sure the finished internal temperature matches the one indicated in the recipe. Poultry often fits in a smaller pot when it's broken down.

→ All my recipes can be scaled down by half, but watch the food carefully to avoid burning because smaller portions will cook faster.

My pot is bigger.

→ Large pots will stay hot longer (due to "carryover cooking") than medium pots will, so check food often and remove the pot from the heat sooner than the recipe suggests.

→ When braising, add more liquid, since there can be more moisture loss when food has more space to cook.

→ Desserts, such as custards, are extremely sensitive to moisture loss, so expect reduced cooking times. Check desserts often, and use a toothpick to help discern doneness.

My pot isn't enameled.

→ Non-enameled Dutch ovens are rougher and more porous than enameled ones. To prevent sticking or tearing of foods, add more oil than called for to coat the pot fully before cooking.

→ Some acidic foods, like tomato, may take on an acrid taste when cooked in a non-enameled pot. Make sure your pot is well seasoned, and remove acidic foods from the pot immediately after cooking to minimize this effect.

Care and Cleaning

If you take care of your Dutch oven, it's likely to last a lifetime. Luckily, you only need to master a few basic guidelines and procedures to maintain these lovely vessels.

1. Don't stack enameled Dutch ovens or store things inside them, because that may cause the enamel to chip.

2. Avoid extreme heat conditions: Each manufacturer provides an upper temperature limit beyond which the pot may sustain damage.

3. Wash your Dutch oven by hand, avoiding abrasive scrubbers. For cleaning, follow these procedures:

Everyday Maintenance

Most Dutch ovens are dishwasher safe, but a dishwasher can dull the finish, and these pots take up a lot of space. Handwashing is best. To clean light messes or mildly caked-on food, soak the pot with water and hand wash with dish soap and a nylon sponge. Never use an abrasive or steel scrubber on enameled pots. It's best to get to the messes the same day. Always let your pot cool fully before cleaning, because a hot pot may crack. After rinsing, store enameled pots with lids ajar to let them dry, and heat non-enameled pots lightly on the stove to eject water from their pores and prevent rust.

Deep Clean

Most enamel-coated Dutch ovens won't require a deep clean, but they may require some elbow grease. With regular use and care, expect a slight amount of permanent staining that won't affect enameled cookware's performance. That said, you may be able to lighten the stain with a mixture of bleach and water or baking soda and water.

Non-enameled cast-iron Dutch ovens will need a deep clean after several uses and will require seasoning (coating with oil) throughout their lives to keep them at peak performance. To deep clean a cast-iron pot, use salt as an abrasive with hot water and scrub vigorously to remove food and old grease.

Seasoning

Enameled Dutch ovens do not need to be seasoned, but non-enameled pots can start to rust or develop dry patches if they are not seasoned regularly. To season a non-enameled cast-iron pot, saturate a paper towel in cooking oil (high-heat vegetable oil, such as avocado, is best) and rub the vessel's inside to apply a thorough coating. Then, heat the vessel over medium heat for a few minutes, turn off the heat, and let the pot cool completely before storing. Do not season the outside of the pot, or it may catch fire when heating. Every time you clean the pot, you will remove some of this oil coating, so season your pot once a week if you cook with it regularly.

DUTCH OVEN PRO TIPS

As you become familiar with Dutch oven cookware, you'll begin to notice how this type of pot behaves differently from other cookware. There are a few best practices to keep in mind.

Preheat your Dutch oven. Cast-iron cookware is slow to warm up, so give it extra time, rather than increasing the heat, to prevent burning food.

Use the right utensils. Use silicone and wooden utensils to protect the coating on enameled cookware. If you have a non-enameled Dutch oven, though, metal tools are fine to use.

Be space conscious. Check the position of your oven racks *before* you preheat the oven. Make sure your pot has room to cook in the center of the oven, unless otherwise specified in the recipe.

Use oven mitts. Dutch oven handles get hot, and you need mitts to manage the pot. Make sure your mitts are dry; wet mitts can steam and burn your hands.

Let it ride. Enamel isn't quite nonstick. If your food is sticking, it probably isn't caramelized enough yet. As long as it isn't burning, let the food cook a little longer before trying to flip it or move it.

Dutch Oven Accessories

The Dutch oven is a minimalist's dream—it's highly functional, and there's little else needed to produce a delicious meal. That said, I want to share some tools that will help you get the most from your pot.

Must Haves

The following tools absolutely make life easier when used in tandem with the Dutch oven. Some or all are required for my recipes.

- **Chef's knife:** An 8- to 10-inch sharp steel blade you will use in every recipe for chopping, mincing, slicing, carving, etc.

- **Colander:** A large bowl-type strainer for draining cooked foods, such as pasta, and rinsing beans and vegetables

- **Ladle:** A long-handled, high-volume spoon for removing and serving hot liquids, sauces, or soups

- **Mixing bowls:** Small, medium, and large bowls, preferably stainless steel, for prep work and mixing

- **Oven mitts:** Thick, padded gloves that protect your hands from the hot handles of your Dutch oven when you move the pot

- **Silicone spatula:** A flexible, flat scraping tool ideal for stirring, lifting, spreading, folding, and sliding under cakes, breads, and rolls; also useful for smoothing batter or frosting

- **Slotted spoon:** A long-handled spoon with holes or mesh for straining liquids, which allows you to transfer food into and out of your pot, leaving the liquids behind (especially useful for transporting vegetables from a pot of soup to the blender)

- **Tongs:** An 8- to 10-inch-long spring-action tool with metal pinchers for lifting or turning roasted or fried food; also great for plucking bay leaves or herb sprigs out of soups or sauces

- **Wooden spoon:** A long-handled, broad, flat spoon used for general stirring, tossing, and flipping

Nice to Haves

In addition to the basic tools you need to cook the Dutch oven recipes in this book, consider adding a few of these time savers, convenience boosters, and specialized tools to your arsenal.

- **Immersion blender:** A handheld blender used to blend foods right in the Dutch oven. Using this tool means you don't have to lift the hot, heavy pot to pour the food into a countertop blender.

- **Kitchen shears:** Very sharp kitchen scissors for cutting large, soft pieces of food (like greens) directly in the pot. Be careful not to scratch the enamel of your pot, and do not use scissors that have been used on nonfood items.

- **Strainer or steamer insert:** A metal basket or perforated plate that elevates food above boiling water, used most commonly for recipes like pot stickers or steamed vegetables. If you have a steamer basket without rubber feet, be careful not to scratch the Dutch oven by scraping the metal feet against the enamel.

- **Thermometers:** Used for checking the internal temperature of meat for correct cooking temperatures and food safety or for regulating oil temperature when deep-frying. These are not strictly necessary with my recipes unless you are using a smaller pot or a larger cut of meat, or if a different cook result is desired. An oven thermometer is a useful tool for calibrating your oven to determine whether it runs hot or cold, and it can help tremendously to test whether or not the recommended cook times are accurate in your oven.

About the Recipes

In the chapters that follow, you will find easy recipes with no more than five steps each to exemplify how your Dutch oven can transform even basic ingredients into a variety of textures, flavors, and cooking experiences. There is an equal blend of classic and contemporary dishes to satisfy traditional and adventurous tastes alike. However, if you are new to Dutch oven cookware, the classic recipes are good starting points to help you discern the features of your pot and learn how this style of cooking differs from using other types of cookware.

General Notes

There are a few things that are true for every recipe. Rather than repeating them, they're assembled here for easy reference.

- **Broth versus stock:** The big difference between broth and stock is salt; broth has it added, while stock doesn't. Most recipes (except any using beef bone broth) call for stock (beef, chicken, or vegetable) because it's unsalted. It's quite easy to add more salt to a recipe, but it's virtually impossible to take it away if there's too much. I recommend seasoning a dish with salt to taste. That said, if broth is what you have on hand, use it, taste it before adding any additional salt, and reduce the amount of additional salt a recipe may call for.

- **Frying:** When heating oil for frying, you want the oil temperature to stay above 350°F throughout the process (if it dips below this temperature, food will be greasy because the oil will seep into the food). Adding cool or room-temperature food to the oil lowers the oil's temperature. To avoid this, I recommend bringing the oil to around 365°F to start, and then frying in small batches. When frying foods, I typically test the oil's temperature using a piece of food. You know the temperature is right when the food in the oil is covered in bubbles and cooks perfectly. Where I've specified batch sizes, those indicate how the food cooks most efficiently and evenly in my moderate-size, enameled Dutch oven.

- **Lukewarm water:** When a recipe calls for lukewarm water, this means a temperature between 90°F and 115°F.

- **Oven temperatures:** Oven temperatures refer to non-convection settings on the center rack, unless otherwise specified. While cook times are offered, please rely on visual cues for best results.

- **Storage:** For food storage, avoid putting the Dutch oven in the refrigerator while it is still hot; if you do, the food will take a very long time to cool. Instead, allow hot food to steam off at room temperature for about 20 minutes, then cover it and store it in the refrigerator. When reheating, remove and reheat just the amount of food you want if you don't plan to finish all of the leftovers (rather than reheating and refrigerating the entire batch of leftovers again).

The Classics ``` CLASSIC ```

This book's classic recipes are iconic dishes most associated with the Dutch oven traditions of stewing, braising, and roasting. After all, the Dutch oven design has changed little over time and continues to capture the rich history of popular fare, such as boeuf bourguignon, coq au vin, and chili. To get started, look for the **classic flag**, which signifies where Dutch oven cooking *has been*.

Contemporary Creations ``` CONTEMPORARY ```

For those who enjoy experimenting with new techniques and flavors, contemporary recipes capture global flavors and food trends, including twists on classics like Kimchi Pot Roast Beef (page 85). These recipes prove the Dutch oven is a multitasker—it fries, bakes, braises, roasts, stores, and chills. You might be surprised to find that deep-dish pizza and ice cream cake are possible with this type of cookware. To shake things up a bit, look for the **contemporary flag**, which signifies where Dutch oven cooking *is headed*.

Other Helpful Labels

You'll find the following icons at the top of applicable recipes.

30-Minute Meal: This icon means the meal can be made from start to finish in 30 minutes or less. You'll find the 30-Minute Meal icon most often on sautés and fried foods.

Dairy-Free   Gluten-Free   Nut-Free

Vegan   Vegetarian

Dietary Labels: The **Dairy-Free, Gluten-Free, Nut-Free, Vegan,** and **Vegetarian icons** will help you seamlessly navigate dietary restrictions or preferences. You can often modify a recipe, too, so check the ingredient tips for recommended substitutions.

ONE POT

One Pot: These no-fuss recipes require a single Dutch oven for all of the cooking steps. Because the point is to streamline cleanup, you'll only need up to one additional bowl and/or cutting board for prep.

BRANDY BERRY FRENCH TOAST CASSEROLE, page 23

Breakfast and Brunch

CHAPTER TWO

Yes, you really can make breakfast in a Dutch oven! Whether you prefer savory or sweet, your favorite start to the day can be done as quickly and easily as anything else in the Dutch oven. Your Dutch oven is a spectacular donut fryer and can even double as a baking pan for cinnamon rolls. And the savory classics? Frittatas, potatoes, eggs—yep, we're doing 'em.

You don't *need* a Dutch oven to cook an omelet, but, once again, the Dutch oven's size is where its convenience lies. You can speedily produce multiple portions of French toast and veggie-loaded hash browns in the Dutch oven by reimagining them as casseroles. These larger-batch recipes store well and are great for brunch parties, where it's important to have all the portions cooked at the same time, or for when you just want to cook once and enjoy quick breakfasts for the next few days. Although you may not use your Dutch oven for single-serve portions, it certainly has value for those times when you want leftovers or are serving four or more people. And, whenever you want a perfectly cooked hard- or soft-boiled egg, your Dutch oven will help you achieve consistent results.

Perfect Hard- or Soft-Boiled Eggs

Serves 4 / **Prep time:** 5 minutes / **Cook time:** 6 to 11 minutes

This foolproof boil-steam method involves cooking eggs quickly in a small amount of boiling water where the tops of the eggs are exposed to steam. I discovered this technique one day when I was in a hurry, and I've been using it ever since because it's so practical. Once the water boils, lower the heat to medium, which will ensure that the eggshells don't crack while they cook.

4 large cold eggs

1. **Boil the water.** For this technique to work perfectly, you only need the eggs to be partially submerged in water. Before adding the eggs, fill a Dutch oven with 1 inch of water and bring the water to a boil over high heat.

2. **Cover and time the eggs.** Lower the temperature to medium, then immediately add the eggs to the pot. Cover the pot and start the timer: 6 minutes for a liquid yolk, 7 to 8 minutes for a jam-like yolk, and 11 minutes for a firm yolk.

3. **Fill a bowl with water and ice.** While the eggs cook, fill a medium bowl with water and ice to create an ice bath. Set aside.

4. **Cool and peel the eggs.** When the timer goes off, immediately transfer the eggs to the ice-water bath. When the eggs are cool, tap each one on the edge of a hard surface to crack the shell. Carefully peel and enjoy, or refrigerate the eggs in their shells for up to 4 days. To keep the texture of the egg yolk, I've found it's best to rewarm eggs in very hot water for a few minutes.

Peanut Butter– Chia Oatmeal

Serves 4 / **Prep time:** 5 minutes / **Cook time:** 3 minutes

Oatmeal is always more enjoyable and nutritious when it's loaded with goodies. Quick cooking oats only take a few minutes in the Dutch oven, so this breakfast is built for speed. You can swirl in as much peanut butter as you want and pile it high with fresh berries and bananas. Chia seeds add a nutritious crunch, especially when sprinkled on at the end.

4 cups water

¼ teaspoon salt

2 cups quick cooking oats

¼ cup creamy peanut butter

1 ripe banana, sliced

4 ounces fresh berries of choice

Chia seeds, for garnish

Honey or brown sugar, for serving (optional)

1. **Boil the water.** In a Dutch oven over high heat, combine the water and salt and bring to a boil.

2. **Cook the oats.** Stir in the oats, reduce the heat to medium, and simmer for 2 minutes, stirring occasionally. Turn off the heat.

3. **Add the peanut butter and serve with fruit.** Stir in the peanut butter. Ladle the oats into serving bowls and garnish with banana slices, berries, and chia seeds. Sweeten with honey or brown sugar (if using). Refrigerate leftover oatmeal for up to 2 days. Add a splash of milk when reheating for a creamy texture.

Turmeric Breakfast Potatoes

Serves 4 / **Prep time:** 10 minutes / **Cook time:** 40 minutes

From the seasoning to the cooking method, these are some truly special breakfast potatoes. The potatoes are boiled until they are half cooked (parboiled), then roasted for an incredibly tender texture with just a bit of golden crust on the outside. Turmeric and smoked paprika give these potatoes oomph, and roasted onion and bell pepper give the dish little pops of sweetness. You can also use 1 tablespoon of minced peeled fresh turmeric root instead of ground turmeric.

3 large Yukon gold
  potatoes, cubed
Pinch salt plus
  ½ teaspoon, divided
1 tablespoon olive oil
1 white onion,
  roughly chopped
1 orange bell pepper,
  roughly chopped
4 garlic cloves, smashed
1 teaspoon
  ground turmeric
½ teaspoon
  smoked paprika
Freshly ground
  black pepper

1. **Preheat the oven.** Preheat the oven to 425°F.

2. **Parboil the potatoes.** Fill a Dutch oven with 1 inch of water. Bring the water to a boil over high heat, add the potatoes and a large pinch of salt, and boil for 3 minutes to cook the potatoes partially (a fork should pierce a piece of potato with some resistance). Place a colander in the sink and drain the potatoes. Let the potatoes sit for a few minutes to steam.

3. **Roast and serve.** Place the Dutch oven over low heat and add the oil, onion, bell pepper, and garlic, tossing to coat. Cook for 2 minutes, stirring frequently to prevent browning. Add the potatoes. Stir well and season with the turmeric, smoked paprika, and the remaining ½ teaspoon of salt. Roast, uncovered, in the oven for 28 minutes. Taste and adjust the seasoning with salt and pepper as desired. Refrigerate leftovers for up to 3 days.

Shakshuka Eggs in Purgatory

Serves 6 / **Prep time:** 5 minutes / **Cook time:** 15 minutes

This popular Middle Eastern breakfast dish, consisting of eggs cooked in a bubbly tomato sauce, takes full advantage of the Dutch oven as a poaching and steaming vessel. Shakshuka comes together in a few minutes on the stovetop and is designed to be served with toast. I like to use a ladle to get a generous scoop of the tomato sauce with each egg and serve it in shallow bowls with fresh herbs.

1 tablespoon olive oil

½ yellow onion, finely chopped

1 red bell pepper, finely chopped

2 (14-ounce) cans fire-roasted diced tomatoes with garlic

2 tablespoons tomato paste

2 teaspoons paprika

1 teaspoon ground cumin

6 large eggs

1 tablespoon finely chopped fresh parsley

Salt

Freshly ground black pepper

Toast, for serving (optional)

1. **Sweat the vegetables and make the sauce.** In a Dutch oven over medium heat, combine the olive oil, onion, and red bell pepper. Cook for about 3 minutes, until soft. Stir in the tomatoes with their juices, tomato paste, paprika, and cumin. Cook for 2 minutes, until slightly reduced.

2. **Cover and cook the eggs in the sauce.** One at a time, gently crack the eggs into the tomato sauce. Cover the pot and set a timer for 6 minutes. Sprinkle fresh parsley over the dish and season with salt and pepper. Serve the saucy eggs with toast (if using) for dipping. Refrigerate leftovers for up to 3 days.

Brandy Berry French Toast Casserole

Serves 6 / **Prep time:** 10 minutes / **Cook time:** 50 minutes

This challah French toast gets its perky, rise-and-shine vibe from a top layer of egg, orange zest, and brandy. Of course, you could hand dip and pan-fry individual slices of bread, but that takes time and, in my experience, means the cook is the last to eat. So, if you want hands-free French toast that you get to sit down and enjoy hot along with everyone else, French toast casserole is the way to go.

Unsalted butter, for preparing the Dutch oven

1 (1-pound) day-old loaf challah bread, sliced

4 large eggs

1¾ cups half-and-half

⅓ cup pure maple syrup, plus more for serving (optional)

1 tablespoon brandy

1 teaspoon grated orange zest

½ teaspoon salt

1½ cups frozen mixed berries

1. **Preheat the oven.** Preheat the oven to 350°F. Generously coat the inside of a Dutch oven with butter.

2. **Assemble and bake the casserole.** Arrange the bread slices in the Dutch oven, overlapping them. In a medium bowl, whisk the eggs, half-and-half, maple syrup, brandy, orange zest, and salt to combine. Add the berries. Pour the egg mixture over the bread, making sure to get the liquid between the slices. Cover the pot and bake for 40 minutes. Remove the lid and cook for 10 minutes more. Serve with maple syrup (if using). Refrigerate leftovers for up to 4 days.

VARIATION TIP: The small amount of alcohol plays a supporting role. If you want to taste more of the brandy, increase the amount to 3 tablespoons, or try 2 teaspoons of vanilla extract in place of the brandy.

Cheesy Green Chile Chilaquiles

Serves 4 / Prep time: 10 minutes / Cook time: 10 minutes

The goal with chilaquiles is to repurpose dry tortillas—so I take more of a visual approach when frying and saucing the tortillas for a combination of crispy, moist, and warm. While you may need a recipe initially, you'll quickly find the process easy enough to remember and adapt on your own. I enjoy chilaquiles best when they are served immediately, because otherwise the tortillas become mushy quickly.

¼ cup refined coconut oil

10 corn tortillas, cut into eighths

Salt

1 (24-ounce) jar salsa verde

½ cup crumbled Cotija cheese

1 tablespoon finely chopped fresh cilantro

¼ cup sour cream

1. **Fry the tortillas.** In a Dutch oven over medium heat, melt the coconut oil. Working in three batches, fry the tortillas, stirring and flipping, for about 1 minute per batch until lightly browned (it's okay if the tortillas overlap a bit). If you see smoke, reduce the heat. Transfer the cooked tortillas to a paper towel–lined plate to drain, and sprinkle with a pinch of salt.

2. **Warm the salsa.** Turn off the heat under the Dutch oven, then add the salsa (it will bubble for a few seconds). When the bubbling stops, place the browned tortillas on top. Do not stir. Turn the heat to medium and cook for 2 minutes. Turn the heat off and sprinkle the cheese over the tortillas. Serve the chilaquiles immediately, garnished with cilantro and sour cream.

SUBSTITUTION TIP: If you can't find Cotija cheese, use a mild shredded cheese such as Monterey Jack.

Goat Cheese and Roasted Bell Pepper Frittata

Serves 6 / **Prep time:** 10 minutes / **Cook time:** 25 minutes

Here, the eggs are cooked partially on the stovetop, as if you're making an omelet, and finished in the oven for one large frittata speckled with bits of roasted bell pepper and goat cheese. Making a frittata is a great way to reflect vegetables' seasonality; you can swap out the peppers for whatever's in season. Enameled Dutch ovens are ideal for cooking a thick, puffy frittata like this one.

12 large eggs

3 tablespoons whole milk

½ teaspoon salt

1 tablespoon olive oil

8 ounces (½ cup) jarred
    roasted bell peppers,
    roughly chopped

4 ounces goat
    cheese, crumbled

1. **Preheat the oven.** Preheat the oven to 425°F.

2. **Whisk the egg mixture.** In a medium bowl, whisk together the eggs, milk, and salt.

3. **Assemble the frittata.** Place the oil in a Dutch oven, then set the pot over medium heat. Add the egg mixture. Cook for about 2 minutes, using a spatula to continuously stir and scrape along the bottom of the pot, until the eggs begin to thicken. Spread the red bell peppers and goat cheese over the top of the frittata before the eggs set. Turn off the heat.

4. **Bake the frittata.** Transfer the Dutch oven to the oven and roast for about 18 minutes, until the eggs are puffy and fully cooked. Let the frittata cool for several minutes, then use a spatula to cut and portion the frittata onto serving plates. Refrigerate leftovers for up to 3 days.

INGREDIENT TIP: You could roast your own red bell peppers, but using jarred peppers saves time and prepared peppers are just as good in this frittata.

Powdered Sugar Beignets

Serves 6 / **Prep time:** 15 minutes, plus 2 hours to rise / **Cook time:** 20 minutes

After visiting New Orleans' French Quarter, I set out to create donuts with a similar texture to the city's famous beignets. I think these are every bit as good as the original. Although the recipe produces a small quantity of dough, you will get about 24 rectangular donuts that expand when cooked. Cook the donuts in batches, and use refined coconut oil if you can because it fries cleanly, has no taste, and produces high-quality donuts.

½ cup lukewarm water

3 tablespoons sugar

1 teaspoon active dry yeast

1 large egg

½ teaspoon salt

3 tablespoons whole milk
or half-and-half

2⅓ cups bread flour, plus
more for dusting

1 tablespoon shortening

4 cups refined coconut oil,
plus more for preparing
the bowl

⅓ cup powdered sugar

1. **Activate the yeast.** Use warm, not scalding, water. In a medium bowl, stir together the lukewarm water, sugar, and yeast. Let the mixture sit for 5 minutes; you should see tiny bubbles begin to form, an indication that the yeast is active. If this happens, proceed with the recipe. If the mixture is not bubbly, the yeast is no longer good; you'll need to get new yeast.

2. **Mix the dough.** Add the egg, salt, and milk to the activated yeast, and gently stir to mix. Add the flour and shortening and stir to form a sticky dough.

3. **Knead the dough.** Sprinkle flour on a work surface and knead the dough for several minutes until it is smooth. Coat a large bowl with coconut oil and put the dough in it. Cover the bowl with a clean cloth and let the dough rise in a warm place for at least 2 hours or until it has doubled in size.

4. **Heat and test the oil.** In a Dutch oven over medium heat, warm the coconut oil. When the oil is hot, add a small piece of dough as a tester. When the tester floats and turns golden, the oil is ready.

5. **Roll the dough and deep-fry it.** Roll the dough into a large, roughly ¼-inch-thick rectangle, then use a pizza cutter or dough scraper to cut it into rows, then rectangles (you're shooting for about 24 rectangles). Working in batches of 5 or 6, gently drop the dough, one piece at a time, into the hot oil. Fry for 1 to 3 minutes, until golden, flipping constantly. Using a slotted spoon, transfer the beignets to a clean paper bag or a large paper towel–lined plate. Dust the beignets with the powdered sugar, hold the bag closed, and shake to coat. The beignets are best served fresh.

Hash Brown Breakfast Casserole

 ONE POT

Serves 6 / Prep time: 10 minutes / Cook time: 1 hour 5 minutes

This egg, hash brown, and sausage casserole is the ultimate savory breakfast. You can use any kind of sausage (or ham) in this recipe, and it's easy to modify the vegetables, too. Generally, if you want to add vegetables that have a lot of moisture, such as mushrooms, cook them down a bit first to reduce their moisture. Slice and serve this casserole for breakfast, or top it with chili to make a hearty dinner.

1 pound ground sausage

½ yellow onion, finely chopped

1 bell pepper, any color, chopped

1 (20-ounce) bag frozen shredded hash browns, thawed

Salt

Freshly ground black pepper

8 large eggs

1⅓ cups whole milk

2 cups shredded cheddar cheese

Pickled jalapeño pepper slices, for garnish (optional)

1. **Preheat the oven.** Preheat the oven to 350°F.

2. **Brown the sausage.** In a Dutch oven over medium heat, cook the sausage for about 4 minutes, stirring to crumble the meat, until browned.

3. **Assemble and bake the casserole.** Turn off the heat and add the onion, bell pepper, and hash browns, tossing to coat with the fat drippings. Season with salt and pepper. In a medium bowl, whisk the eggs and milk until smooth. Pour the egg mixture over the hash brown casserole and top with the cheese and jalapeños (if using). Bake for 1 hour or until cooked through. Serve warm. Refrigerate leftovers for up to 3 days.

MAKE IT CONTEMPORARY: This is a fun recipe to use fresh herbs or your favorite spice blends in—everything bagel, Cajun, Italian, etc. If you don't have jalapeños and you like your food spicy, add a dash of hot sauce or cayenne pepper.

Chorizo Breakfast Burritos

Serves 6 / Prep time: 5 minutes / Cook time: 15 minutes

This burrito recipe exemplifies how you might use a single Dutch oven to prepare multiple components of a dish. I like to warm the tortillas in the oven while I cook each component separately so I'm ready to rock and roll as soon as the tortillas are pliable. Before you get cooking, set holding bowls near the Dutch oven for the chorizo, hash browns, and scrambled eggs. Once the tortillas and filling are ready, I like to make a quick practice roll first so I know how much filling should go in each burrito.

6 (12-inch or larger)
   flour tortillas
2 tablespoons canola
   oil, divided
1 pound chorizo
½ yellow onion,
   finely chopped
Salt
1 cup shredded frozen
   hash browns
Freshly ground
   black pepper
8 large eggs
1 cup shredded
   cheddar cheese
Salsa, for serving

1. **Preheat the oven and warm the tortillas.** Preheat the oven to 300°F. Spread the tortillas on a baking sheet, overlapping. Bake for 10 to 15 minutes to warm the tortillas.

2. **Cook and drain the chorizo.** In a Dutch oven over medium heat, warm 1 tablespoon of canola oil. Add the chorizo, onion, and a pinch of salt. Cook for about 4 minutes, stirring occasionally, until browned. Using a slotted spoon, scoop the chorizo and onion into a bowl.

3. **Crisp the hash browns.** Return the pot to the heat and add the remaining 1 tablespoon of canola oil. Add the hash browns, spreading them in the pot, and fry for 5 minutes, until crispy and browned on the bottom. Avoid stirring the hash browns so they brown better. Flip the hash browns, season with salt and pepper, and cook for 3 minutes more. Transfer to a small bowl. Set aside.

CONTINUED >

4. **Scramble the eggs.** Return the pot to the heat and add the eggs. Cook for 2 to 3 minutes, stirring frequently to scramble the eggs. Season with salt and pepper, then turn off the heat.

5. **Assemble the burritos.** Spoon some of the chorizo, hash browns, and eggs onto each tortilla. Sprinkle with the cheese. Fold the tortillas, tucking in the sides, and roll them up into burritos. Enjoy them warm with salsa on the side. Refrigerate leftovers for up to 4 days, or freeze them in sealed bags for up to 2 months.

Cinnamon Rolls with Cream Cheese Frosting

Serves 8 / **Prep time:** 20 minutes, plus 1 hour 30 minutes to rise / **Cook time:** 30 minutes

You don't need any special tools to make perfect cinnamon rolls at home, just a lively round of kneading and some time as the dough rises. Your patience will be rewarded with warm, cream cheese–frosted heaven. Trust me, you don't want to make these rolls if you're home alone, but if you feel like taking your chances, you can freeze the cinnamon rolls and reheat them at your own pace.

FOR THE DOUGH

1 (0.25-ounce) packet
   active dry yeast
   (2¼ teaspoons)
½ cup lukewarm water
½ cup whole milk
¼ cup sugar
5 tablespoons plus
   1 teaspoon cold
   unsalted butter
1 teaspoon salt
1 large egg
3⅓ cups all-purpose
   flour, divided, plus more
   for dusting

FOR THE FILLING

¾ cup packed light
   brown sugar
8 tablespoons (1 stick)
   unsalted butter, melted
2 tablespoons
   ground cinnamon

1. **Preheat the oven.** Preheat the oven to 350°F.

2. **Make the dough.** In a small bowl, gently stir together the yeast and lukewarm water. Set aside for 5 minutes or until you see tiny bubbles form on the surface. In a small microwave-safe bowl, microwave the milk on high heat for 90 seconds to scald it. Transfer the milk to a large bowl and stir in the sugar, butter, salt, and egg (small butter lumps are okay). Stir in 1 cup of flour, then the yeast mixture. Add the remaining 2⅓ cups of flour. Dust a work surface with flour and turn the dough out onto it. Knead the dough for 5 minutes. Cover the dough and let it rise at room temperature for about 1 hour, until doubled in size.

3. **Roll and cut the rolls and make the filling.** Flatten the dough with your palms to form a large, ½-inch-thick rectangle. In a small bowl, stir together the brown sugar, melted butter, and cinnamon to form a grainy paste. Evenly spread the cinnamon-sugar mixture across the dough. Starting from a long edge, roll the dough into a log, pinching together the edges to seal. Cut the log into 8 roughly equal-size pieces.

CONTINUED >

FOR THE FROSTING

6 ounces cream cheese

5 tablespoons plus
   1 teaspoon cold
   unsalted butter

1 teaspoon vanilla extract

2 cups powdered sugar

4. **Rise, then bake.** Arrange the cinnamon rolls close together in a Dutch oven. Cover the pot and let the rolls rise for 30 minutes at room temperature. Bake, uncovered, for 30 minutes or until the rolls are lightly golden brown. Remove from the oven and let cool.

5. **Frost and serve.** In a medium microwave-safe bowl, combine the cream cheese and butter. Warm in the microwave on high power for 50 seconds. Cut the butter with a fork, then stir until the mixture is smooth and glossy. Add the vanilla and stir in the powdered sugar, a bit at a time, to form a thick frosting. Spread the frosting over the slightly cooled rolls, and serve warm. Refrigerate leftovers for up to 3 days, or freeze them in an airtight bag for up to 2 months.

TECHNICAL TIP: You don't have to grease the work surface when you roll out the dough, but you can if you want to. Because this is a butter dough, it's not terribly sticky, so I like to use my fingertips to peel the dough away from the counter as I roll it. It releases very easily and makes less of a mess that way.

SESAME-GINGER SOBA NOODLE SALAD, page 46

Pasta, Rice, and Other Grains

CHAPTER THREE

Grains and pasta make ideal pantry staples because they are shelf stable and incredibly convenient. Pasta, especially, has become an essential component of American cooking, largely because it is so easy to prepare. But rice and other grains are every bit as quick and easy in the Dutch oven, making them just as practical for busy weeknight dinners. Just start cooking some aromatic brown rice with olive oil, fresh herbs, garlic, and cheese, and you'll be sitting down to a nutritious meal shortly after.

Think of this chapter and its recipes as blueprints for myriad meal variations featuring pantry staples. Master a handful of ways to cook grains, and pair them with seasonal sauces or sides for complete dishes. For instance, make your own pesto sauce in the short time it takes to cook rigatoni, and sit down to a refreshing summer meal. When chilly weather demands something warm and robust, throw together a thick Salmon Congee with Sesame (page 40), or make Parmesan Polenta with Thyme-Roasted Mushrooms (page 42). In the spring, serve cold soba noodles with a light, cleansing ginger stock and crunchy vegetables.

Perhaps my favorite way to use a Dutch oven is to slowly cook rice or pasta to break down the starches and develop deeper flavors. For example, when you add dried pasta to a soupy sauce, you end up with an incredibly satisfying goulash.

Ginger-Scented Rice

Serves 6 / **Prep time:** 10 minutes / **Cook time:** 1 hour 15 minutes

When you cook rice slowly in a Dutch oven over a campfire, you get this golden, nutty brown layer along the bottom. That treasured crispy rice crust is the inspiration for this recipe, where the rice cooks slowly in the oven. For really fluffy rice, use boiling-hot water. I like to add a small amount of coconut oil to keep the rice slick and prevent sticking, plus some fresh ginger for its lovely aroma and flavor.

1 cup brown basmati rice

2 teaspoons unrefined
coconut oil

2¼ cups boiling water

½ teaspoon salt

1 (1-inch) piece fresh
ginger, halved

1. **Preheat the oven.** Preheat the oven to 375°F.

2. **Rinse the rice.** Place the rice in a medium bowl, then fill the bowl with water. Swirl the rice with your hands. Drain.

3. **Dry the rice and add the oil.** In a Dutch oven over medium heat, cook the rice, stirring, for about 3 minutes or until the grains are dry. Add the coconut oil and stir to coat the rice.

4. **Add the water and cook the rice.** Add the boiling water, salt, and ginger. Cover the pot and bake for about 1 hour, until all the water is absorbed.

5. **Steam and fluff the rice.** Remove the pot and let the rice steam, covered, for 10 minutes. Using a spatula, fluff the rice. Remove and discard the ginger before serving.

VARIATION TIP: Instead of coconut oil, add 1 tablespoon of unsalted butter for a richer flavor.

Lemony Quinoa and Kale Salad

Serves 4 / **Prep time:** 15 minutes / **Cook time:** 35 minutes

This nutty and fresh salad is full of pine nuts, black olives, and tomatoes. I've been making it for a decade and love the way the lemon provides a zesty summertime quality. It's great for picnic lunches because the kale will hold its shape and texture when transported or kept out for a bit. I like to mix this salad in a large bowl while the quinoa cooks, then fluff the grains and fold them in last. Use boiling water for fluffy grains and cold for sticky ones.

¼ cup olive oil, plus more for seasoning

2 tablespoons pine nuts

2 garlic cloves, minced

¼ teaspoon red pepper flakes

1 cup white quinoa

1 teaspoon salt, divided

1¾ cups boiling water

Juice of 3 lemons, plus more for seasoning

1 (2.25-ounce) can sliced black olives, drained

1 bunch curly kale, ribbed and roughly chopped

1 bunch fresh parsley, finely chopped

4 Roma tomatoes, seeded and chopped

1. **Infuse the oil and make the sauce.** In a Dutch oven over medium heat, combine the olive oil, pine nuts, garlic, and red pepper flakes. Warm for about 2 minutes, just until the pine nuts begin to lightly brown, then transfer the mixture to a large bowl and set aside.

2. **Rinse and cook the quinoa.** Place the quinoa in a fine-mesh sieve, and rinse it well. Transfer the quinoa to the Dutch oven; add ½ teaspoon of salt and the boiling water. Place the pot over high heat and bring the water back to a boil. Reduce the heat to low, cover the pot, and simmer for 15 minutes. Remove from the heat and let the quinoa steam, covered, for 10 minutes.

3. **Make the kale salad.** Add the lemon juice and the remaining ½ teaspoon of salt to the bowl with the olive oil and pine nuts. Stir well, then add the black olives, kale, parsley, and tomatoes, tossing to coat. Using a fork, fluff the quinoa, then, a bit at a time, mix it into the kale salad. Taste and adjust the seasoning, adding extra lemon juice, olive oil, or salt as desired. Serve cold or at room temperature. Refrigerate leftovers, which keep very well, for up to 4 days.

Spanakorizo

Serves 6 / Prep time: 10 minutes / Cook time: 1 hour

This Greek spinach and rice pilaf is a unique spin on a side dish that involves cooking the rice in water infused with scallion, lemon, and dill. During the steaming period, raw spinach gets folded into the rice, resulting in a moist texture, similar to risotto. This rice is nice and creamy with a tangy flavor, and it makes the perfect accompaniment to fish.

½ cup olive oil

1 yellow or white
onion, chopped

6 scallions, thinly sliced

1 cup medium-grain
brown rice

¼ cup freshly squeezed
lemon juice

1 tablespoon finely
chopped fresh dill

1 teaspoon salt

2½ cups water

1 pound fresh
baby spinach

1. **Sweat the onions.** In a Dutch oven over medium heat, heat the olive oil. Add the onion and scallions and sweat for about 8 minutes until soft, stirring occasionally.

2. **Cook the rice.** Stir in the rice, lemon juice, dill, salt, and water. Bring to a boil over high heat. Cover the pot, reduce the heat to medium-low, and simmer for 40 minutes, or until most of the water is absorbed.

3. **Stir in the spinach.** Turn off the heat and stir in the spinach. Re-cover the pot and let steam for 10 minutes. Transfer the pilaf to a serving platter. Refrigerate leftovers for up to 4 days.

Salmon Congee with Sesame

Serves 6 / **Prep time:** 10 minutes / **Cook time:** 45 minutes

Making congee involves overcooking rice in water to create a thick, creamy soup. Chicken is more traditional, but this variation with salmon, sesame seeds, and chives is especially striking and well balanced in flavor. Sesame seeds are sold toasted or raw; if you find them toasted, skip the first step. I especially love how beautiful black sesame seeds look against the white rice.

¼ cup sesame seeds

4½ cups water

½ cup white basmati rice

1½ teaspoons salt

8 ounces fresh salmon fillet, skin removed, cut into 1-inch pieces

1 tablespoon unsalted butter

1 tablespoon toasted sesame oil

½ cup thinly sliced fresh chives

1. **Toast the sesame seeds.** If your seeds are toasted, skip this step. Warm a Dutch oven over medium heat. Add the sesame seeds and cook for about 4 minutes, stirring occasionally, until they have a nutty smell and crunchy texture. Remove the seeds from the pot and set them aside.

2. **Cook the rice.** Combine the water, rice, and salt in the Dutch oven over high heat. Bring to a boil. Turn the heat to medium to maintain a simmer and cook, stirring frequently, for about 30 minutes or until the liquid is creamy and the rice is tender.

3. **Add the salmon.** Stir in the salmon, butter, and sesame oil. Cover the pot and cook for 5 minutes, until the salmon is pink and opaque.

4. **Season and serve.** Stir in the chives, then ladle the congee into bowls. Garnish with a generous pinch of the toasted sesame seeds. Refrigerate leftovers for up to 3 days.

INGREDIENT TIP: If you buy sesame seeds in a labeled container, look for the words "toasted" or "roasted." Raw seeds are flat and chewy; toasted seeds are incredibly crunchy and have an intense, nutty flavor.

Rigatoni with Pumpkin Seed Pesto

Serves 6 / Prep time: 2 minutes / Cook time: 20 minutes

When you want an uncomplicated dinner that still packs a punch, a good pesto tossed with pasta does the trick. To give the pesto umami flavor, I use Pecorino Romano, a hard cheese with a strong, funky flavor. I like to get the pasta going while I make the pesto in the blender, so dinner's on the table in about 20 minutes.

1 teaspoon salt, plus more for seasoning

1 pound rigatoni pasta

1 cup raw pumpkin seeds

5 ounces fresh baby spinach and kale mix

3 garlic cloves, roughly chopped

1 ounce Pecorino Romano cheese, roughly chopped

½ cup olive oil

½ cup red wine vinegar

1 teaspoon red pepper flakes

Freshly ground black pepper

1. **Cook the pasta.** Fill a Dutch oven three-fourths full with water, and place it over high heat. When the water comes to a boil, add several large pinches of salt and the rigatoni. Cook for 10 to 14 minutes, until the pasta is al dente. Place a colander in the sink, and drain the pasta.

2. **Meanwhile, make the pesto.** In a blender or food processor, combine the pumpkin seeds, spinach and kale mix, garlic, Pecorino Romano, olive oil, vinegar, red pepper flakes, and salt. Blend on high speed until the mixture is mostly creamy with a bit of texture.

3. **Sauce the noodles.** Transfer the noodles to a large serving bowl. Add the pesto. Toss to coat. Taste and season with salt and pepper as desired. Refrigerate leftovers for up to 2 days.

VARIATION TIP: Pesto is highly adaptable—as long as you maintain the same ratio of ½ cup olive oil to ½ cup vinegar, mix and match different leafy greens, nuts, and seeds. Try walnut with arugula and a handful of fresh basil.

Parmesan Polenta with Thyme-Roasted Mushrooms

Serves 4 / **Prep time:** 15 minutes / **Cook time:** 30 minutes

You can serve polenta several ways. When it's fully cooked, it has a thick, porridge-like consistency. This is how I like to serve it with shrimp (think shrimp and grits). However, if you let the polenta cool completely, it firms up beautifully and can be sliced and fried, baked, or grilled. Roasting the mushrooms on top of the polenta elevates the umami flavor I always seek to bring out in my cooking.

2½ cups vegetable stock

1 teaspoon
 balsamic vinegar

½ teaspoon salt, plus
 more for seasoning

¾ cup polenta corn grits

½ cup finely grated
 Parmesan cheese

8 ounces cremini
 mushrooms, thinly sliced

8 ounces shiitake
 mushrooms, thinly sliced

Leaves from 4 thyme
 sprigs, or 1 teaspoon
 dried thyme

2 tablespoons olive oil

Pinch red pepper flakes,
 for seasoning (optional)

1. **Preheat the oven.** Preheat the oven to 450°F.

2. **Cook the polenta.** In a Dutch oven over high heat, combine the vegetable stock, vinegar, and salt. Bring to a boil. Add the polenta and stir well. Lower the heat to maintain a simmer and cook for 10 minutes, stirring often, until creamy and tender. Remove from the heat and stir in the Parmesan. Smooth the top of the polenta and set aside to firm.

3. **Roast the polenta with the mushrooms.** In a medium bowl, stir together the cremini and shiitake mushrooms, thyme, olive oil, and a large pinch of salt. Spread the mushroom mixture over the polenta. Roast for about 15 minutes, until the mushrooms are tender. Using a spatula, cut the polenta into portions and serve with the mushrooms and the red pepper flakes (if using). Refrigerate leftovers for up to 3 days.

INGREDIENT TIP: When shopping for polenta, look for coarsely ground yellow corn grits—these bags are often labeled "polenta." To clarify, there is a breakfast cereal called "grits" that is not the same as polenta; it is made from a finer grind of white corn.

Italian Beef and Tomato Goulash

 ONE POT

Serves 6 / Prep time: 10 minutes / Cook time: 40 minutes

My idea of "one pot" is epitomized in this classic Dutch oven goulash. It demands very little effort yet yields big, comforting results of beef, pasta, tomato, and cheese. There's no need to pre-cook the macaroni because it will cook in the sauce. Once you add the pasta, though, it's important to stir every so often to prevent the food from scorching along the bottom of the pot.

2 pounds lean ground beef

2 garlic cloves, minced

2 tablespoons Italian seasoning

1 teaspoon salt

½ teaspoon freshly ground black pepper

1 (14.5-ounce) can diced tomatoes

1 (26-ounce) jar pasta sauce

3 cups water

3 tablespoons tamari

2 cups dried elbow macaroni

1 cup shredded cheddar cheese

1. **Cook the beef.** In a Dutch oven over medium heat, cook the ground beef for 5 minutes, crumbling it with a spatula or wooden spoon, until mostly cooked through. Stir in the garlic, Italian seasoning, salt, and pepper. Cook for 2 minutes.

2. **Add the liquids.** Add the tomatoes and their juices, pasta sauce, water, and tamari. Stir, cover the pot, and simmer for 10 minutes.

3. **Cook the pasta in the sauce.** Stir in the macaroni. Cover the pot and simmer for about 20 minutes, until the pasta is just cooked, stirring every few minutes to prevent the noodles from sticking and burning.

4. **Add the cheese and serve.** Stir in the cheddar cheese and serve. The goulash reheats well. Refrigerate leftovers for up to 4 days.

VARIATION TIP: Shoyu and soy sauce are both good substitutes for tamari.

Beef Stroganoff

Serves 6 / Prep time: 15 minutes / Cook time: 15 minutes

Before I knew how to cook, I practiced with beef stroganoff. My problem, at first, was that the sauce would dry out by the time I served the noodles. After making this dish over and over, I finally realized that if the freshly drained noodles hit the sauce right around the time the sauce is done, the texture is glorious. To get the best texture, I recommend reading the recipe first to help you synchronize the noodles and sauce.

Salt

4 tablespoons (½ stick) unsalted butter, divided

2 pounds lean ground beef

Freshly ground black pepper

1 pound egg noodles

1 yellow onion, finely chopped

4 garlic cloves, minced

1 pound cremini mushrooms, sliced

½ cup dry white wine

1 tablespoon Worcestershire sauce

½ cup sour cream

Finely chopped fresh parsley, for garnish (optional)

1. **Boil the water.** Bring a large pot of salted water to a boil over high heat.

2. **Cook the beef.** Meanwhile, in a Dutch oven over medium heat, melt 2 tablespoons of butter. Add the ground beef and season well with salt and pepper. Cook for 4 minutes, crumbling the beef with a spatula or wooden spoon, until brown. Transfer the beef with its juices to a large bowl; set aside.

3. **Cook the pasta.** Add the egg noodles to the boiling water and cook for 8 to 10 minutes, until al dente. Place a colander in the sink, and drain the pasta; do not rinse the noodles.

4. **While the pasta cooks, sauté the vegetables.** In a Dutch oven over medium heat, melt the remaining 2 tablespoons of butter. Add the onion and sauté for about 3 minutes. Stir in the garlic and mushrooms. Sauté for about 5 minutes, until the onion and mushrooms are soft and beginning to brown. Pour the wine over the vegetables and stir well, scraping along the bottom of the pot to release any browned bits.

5. **Mix the beef with the vegetables and serve.**
Return the beef with its juices to the pot and stir in the Worcestershire sauce and sour cream. Immediately serve the warm beef sauce over the just-cooked noodles and garnish with parsley (if using). Taste and adjust the seasoning with salt and pepper as desired. Refrigerate leftovers for up to 3 days. When reheating, add a splash of water to thin the sauce.

TECHNICAL TIP: For a thicker sauce, make a quick roux by adding 2 tablespoons of all-purpose flour *after* sautéing the vegetables. Cook, stirring, for at least 3 minutes to toast the flour, then proceed with the wine and other liquids. Once the sauce comes to a simmer, it will thicken into a gravy.

Sesame-Ginger Soba Noodle Salad

Serves 4 / **Prep time:** 10 minutes / **Cook time:** 20 minutes

These sesame noodles make a simple side dish or main meal served hot or cold. Soba noodles are made from buckwheat flour and can be purchased with or without wheat added. You can use a variety of vegetables in this dish, but I especially like the meatiness of shiitake mushrooms.

Salt

8 ounces gluten-free
   soba noodles

¼ cup sesame oil

8 ounces shiitake
   mushrooms, thinly sliced

2 heads bok choy, cut into
   ½-inch-thick slices

2 teaspoons peeled and
   minced fresh ginger

1 teaspoon red
   pepper flakes

¼ cup tamari

¼ cup rice vinegar

2 tablespoons brown
   rice syrup

2 tablespoons mirin

1. **Cook the pasta.** Bring a Dutch oven filled with salted water to a boil over high heat. Add the soba noodles and cook according to the package instructions. Place a colander in the sink, drain the noodles, and rinse them under cold water. Set aside.

2. **Cook the vegetables and make the sauce.** Combine the sesame oil and shiitake mushrooms in the Dutch oven over medium-low heat. Cook, undisturbed, for 3 minutes. Stir in the bok choy, ginger, and red pepper flakes. Sauté for 1 minute, then add the tamari, vinegar, brown rice syrup, and mirin. Stir to form a smooth sauce, then add the noodles, just tossing to coat. Serve warm or cool.

TECHNICAL TIP: You can tell when the soba noodles are fully cooked by breaking a noodle in half. If you see any white starch, continue to cook the noodles until that starch is no longer visible.

Gouda-Cheddar Mac and Cheese

Serves 6 / **Prep time:** 15 minutes / **Cook time:** 40 minutes

My neighbor used to make the best macaroni and cheese. She used the big macaroni noodles and baked it in this yellow bowl we dubbed "the mac and cheese bowl." Over the years, I acquired bits and pieces of her recipe and adapted them to the Dutch oven. I like to reserve some of the cheddar for topping the macaroni, and I crisp it under the broiler for a few minutes until brown and bubbly.

5 ounces Gouda cheese

5 ounces sharp cheddar cheese

Salt

1 pound large dried elbow macaroni

1 tablespoon olive oil

5 tablespoons unsalted butter

⅓ cup all-purpose flour

2½ cups whole milk

2 teaspoons paprika (optional)

1. **Preheat the oven and prepare the cheeses.** Preheat the oven to 375°F. Shred the Gouda and cheddar cheeses and mix them together in a large bowl. Set aside.

2. **Cook the pasta.** Fill a Dutch oven three-fourths full with salted water and bring it to a boil over high heat. Add the pasta and cook for 1 minute shy of al dente, according to the package instructions. Place a colander in the sink and drain the pasta. Add the olive oil and toss the pasta to prevent sticking.

3. **Make a roux and simmer the milk.** Place the butter in the Dutch oven and set the pot over medium-low heat. When the butter has melted, add the flour and cook, stirring frequently, for 2 minutes or until the mixture is golden and bubbly. Slowly stir in the milk, bring the mixture to a simmer (it will thicken), and then turn off the heat.

4. **Mix in the cheese and pasta.** Add the cheese and pasta to the milk mixture, folding well to evenly coat the pasta. Sprinkle the top with the paprika (if using). Bake for about 15 minutes, until golden and bubbly. Serve immediately. Refrigerate leftovers for up to 3 days.

BLACK BEAN SOUP WITH CITRUS, page 57

Soups, Stews, and Chilis

CHAPTER FOUR

I hope these soups, stews, and chilis are a source of welcoming warmth as you ground yourself in the tradition of Dutch oven cooking. No matter the season, you can find comfort in a bowl. Whether light and brothy, creamy and rich, or hearty and thick, each has a place in Dutch oven cooking. Since stewing involves building base layers of flavors, there's quite a bit of room for flexibility, making these recipes particularly easy and adaptable. Using aromatics, caramelization, and stock as a unifying foundation of flavor, try whatever vegetables are in season, experiment with different spices, and create your signature bowl with whatever toppings you crave.

Tomato Bisque with Shrimp

Serves 6 / **Prep time:** 10 minutes / **Cook time:** 20 minutes

This quick bisque is like a thick tomato soup with shrimp, as opposed to a traditional shrimp bisque, which requires a more involved seafood stock. With modern enameled Dutch ovens, it's possible to create acidic soups without a metallic taste from the cast iron. You could use cream to enrich the soup, but I like the subtle flavor of full-fat canned coconut milk with the shrimp.

3 tablespoons olive oil

**1 yellow onion,
   roughly chopped**

**2 celery stalks,
   roughly chopped**

2 teaspoons sea salt

**1 teaspoon freshly ground
   black pepper**

1 garlic clove, minced

1 teaspoon paprika

**1 (28-ounce) can whole
   peeled tomatoes**

**1 (14-ounce) can full-fat
   coconut milk**

**8 ounces fresh shrimp,
   peeled and deveined**

1. **Sweat the vegetables.** Heat the olive oil in a Dutch oven over medium heat. Add the onion, celery, salt, and pepper. Sauté for about 4 minutes or until tender, stirring occasionally. Add the garlic. Cook for 1 minute, stirring frequently. Add the paprika. Cook the onion mixture with the paprika for 1 minute, until fragrant.

2. **Add the liquids.** Add the tomatoes with their juices and the coconut milk. Cover the pot and simmer for 5 minutes. Turn off the heat.

3. **Blend the soup and poach the shrimp.** Using an immersion blender, blend the soup until smooth. Alternatively, working in batches, carefully transfer the soup to a regular blender and blend on high speed until very smooth. Return the soup to the pot. While the soup is still piping hot, add the shrimp and stir. Cook the shrimp in the hot soup for 2 to 3 minutes or until it is pink and white and fully cooked. Ladle the soup into bowls. Refrigerate leftover soup for up to 3 days.

MAKE IT CLASSIC: If you want to intensify the seafood flavor for a more classic shrimp bisque, use 2 cups of seafood stock and reduce the amount of tomatoes by half.

Creamy Broccoli Soup

Serves 6 / **Prep time:** 10 minutes / **Cook time:** 25 minutes

This lightened-up broccoli soup uses the starch in a potato and a quick round of blending to achieve a smooth mouthfeel. Adding the broccoli in the beginning dulls the color, so I like to wait until the end of cooking to preserve some of the vegetable's vibrancy. You can even use frozen broccoli to save some time. For an even richer flavor, add a splash of heavy cream or half-and-half at step 4 with as much cheese as you like. Cheddar is traditional, but Parmesan works equally well.

¼ cup olive oil

½ white onion, chopped

2 celery stalks, chopped

2 carrots, chopped

2½ teaspoons salt

1 small russet
   potato, chopped

2 garlic cloves, minced

4 cups vegetable stock

1 large head broccoli,
   chopped (5 cups florets)

½ cup shredded cheddar
   cheese (optional)

1. **Sweat the vegetables.** Heat a Dutch oven over medium heat. Add the olive oil, onion, celery, carrots, and salt. Sauté for 3 minutes, stirring occasionally to prevent browning.

2. **Cook the potato.** Add the potato and garlic. Sauté for about 7 minutes or until the potato softens and cooks through, stirring occasionally.

3. **Simmer and blend with the broccoli.** Add the vegetable stock, increase the heat to medium-high, and bring the soup to a simmer. Cook for 8 minutes. Turn off the heat and use a slotted spoon to transfer the cooked vegetables to a blender. Scoop out about 2 cups of liquid from the pot and add it to the blender. Add the broccoli florets to the blender and blend on high speed until the mixture is very smooth and creamy.

4. **Return the creamy soup to the pot and serve.** Pour the blended soup back into the Dutch oven and bring it to a simmer. Stir well, then turn off the heat to preserve the broccoli's color. You can add cheddar cheese (if using) to the soup in the Dutch oven, or you can serve the soup and garnish with the cheese. Refrigerate leftovers in the Dutch oven for easy reheating for up to 3 days.

Vegetable and Lentil Soup

Serves 6 / **Prep time:** 10 minutes / **Cook time:** 25 minutes

This simple dish draws a lot of bold flavor from garam masala, a blend of toasted spices. Spices cooked down with vegetables and lentils are all you need to turn simple ingredients into a meal. Although there are many varieties of lentils, it's best to use either red or yellow lentils here because both types cook quickly, usually in 15 to 20 minutes. I like to serve this soup with tahini sauce (sesame seed paste mixed with lemon juice) and a dash of either Aleppo pepper or smoked paprika.

3 tablespoons olive oil

1 onion, chopped

2 carrots, chopped

2 celery stalks, chopped

1 tablespoon garam masala, plus more for seasoning

1 tablespoon salt, plus more for seasoning

2 teaspoons curry powder, plus more for seasoning

1 teaspoon freshly ground black pepper, plus more for seasoning

6 cups filtered water

2 cups red or yellow lentils

1. **Sweat the vegetables.** In a Dutch oven over medium heat, warm the olive oil. Add the onion, carrots, and celery. Sweat the vegetables for 7 minutes, stirring occasionally. Stir in the garam masala, salt, curry powder, and pepper. Cook for about 2 minutes, until aromatic.

2. **Simmer the lentils.** Pour the water over the vegetables and add the lentils. Stir, then cover the pot and simmer, stirring occasionally, for about 15 minutes, until the lentils are tender and cooked through.

3. **Adjust the seasoning and serve.** Taste the soup and add more salt or spices as desired. Ladle the soup into bowls and top as desired. Refrigerate leftovers for up to 3 days.

INGREDIENT TIP: If you can't find garam masala, use a blend of 2 teaspoons of ground cumin, ¼ teaspoon of ground cinnamon, and 1 teaspoon of ground coriander instead.

Cauliflower-Leek Potage

Serves 6 / Prep time: 10 minutes / Cook time: 45 minutes

Meet my go-to Thanksgiving appetizer. This soup is thick, creamy, cozy, and really easy to make. For ultimate convenience, cook it up to three days ahead and freeze portions in sealed plastic bags. The luxurious texture of blended cauliflower and the unexpected dimension of nutty almond-infused brown butter are what make this soup extraordinary.

1 head cauliflower, cut into florets

1 tablespoon sea salt, plus more as needed

Juice of 1 lemon, divided

2 leeks

2 tablespoons olive oil

4 cups vegetable stock

Freshly ground black pepper

4 tablespoons (½ stick) unsalted butter

¼ cup slivered almonds

Freshly grated nutmeg, for seasoning

1. **Boil and drain the cauliflower.** Fill a Dutch oven about halfway with water and add the cauliflower, salt, and the juice of ½ a lemon. Bring to a boil and cook for 15 minutes. Place a colander in the sink and drain the cauliflower.

2. **Sweat the leeks and simmer with stock.** Remove the leeks' tough outer green portions. Cut lengthwise down the center of the white stalks but keep the root ends intact. Fan the leeks under running water to wash away any sand. Thinly slice the leeks and discard the roots. In a Dutch oven over medium heat, heat the olive oil. Add the leeks with a pinch of salt. Cook for 15 minutes until very tender, stirring occasionally to prevent browning. Add the cooked cauliflower and vegetable stock and bring to a simmer.

3. **Blend.** Using a slotted spoon, carefully transfer the leeks and cauliflower to a blender. Using a liquid measuring cup, transfer 1 cup of cooking liquid to the blender. Blend on high speed until very smooth. Return the puree to the Dutch oven. Taste and season with salt and pepper. Spritz with the juice of the remaining ½ lemon.

4. **Brown the butter with the almonds.** In a small skillet over medium-low heat, combine the butter and almonds. Cook for about 5 minutes, stirring occasionally, until the nuts turn lightly golden and the butter is browned. Pour the browned butter into the soup, reserving the almonds for garnish. Swirl the butter into the soup. Ladle into bowls and garnish with almonds for crunch and a dash of nutmeg, preferably freshly grated. Refrigerate leftovers for up to 4 days, or let the soup cool and then freeze it in freezer-safe plastic bags for up to 2 months.

VARIATION TIP: Although I love the intensity of browned butter, sometimes I toast the nuts in olive oil to make this soup dairy free and vegan. If you have an allergy to nuts, use raw pumpkin seeds instead of almonds.

Pork Green Chili

Serves 6 / Prep time: 10 minutes / Cook time: 1 hour 40 minutes

This fun green chili is loaded with complex flavors from the slow-cooked pork shoulder, aromatic spices, and tangy, spicy green chiles. It's an easy restaurant-quality dish I love to show off when cooking for family or friends. As with most chilis, leftovers taste even better, making this a great way to enjoy more home-cooked meals during the week. I prefer shredded mozzarella, cilantro, or queso blanco as a garnish for this recipe.

2 tablespoons olive oil

2 pounds boneless
   pork shoulder

2 teaspoons salt

1 teaspoon dried oregano

1 teaspoon ground cumin

1 teaspoon onion powder

1 teaspoon
   ground coriander

1 cup salsa verde

½ cup sour cream

1 (4-ounce) can diced
   green chiles

1 cup filtered water

1 (15-ounce) can black
   beans, drained
   and rinsed

1. **Cook the pork.** Cut the pork shoulder into cubes, roughly 1 inch thick. In a Dutch oven over medium heat, warm the olive oil. Add the pork and season with the salt. Sear for 3 minutes to brown the meat on all sides, turning it with a spatula.

2. **Add the spices and other ingredients, then simmer.** Stir in the oregano, cumin, onion powder, and coriander. Cook for 30 seconds, until aromatic. Pour in the salsa verde, sour cream, green chiles, and water. Stir to combine, scraping along the bottom of the pot with a wooden spoon or spatula to release any browned bits. Cover the pot and reduce the heat to medium-low. Simmer the soup for 1½ hours or until the pork is tender and shreds easily with a fork.

3. **Add the black beans, adjust seasonings, and serve.** Add the black beans and bring the soup back to a simmer. Taste and adjust the seasoning as desired. Ladle into bowls and garnish with cilantro (if using) and cheese (if using). Refrigerate leftovers for up to 4 days.

Black Bean Soup with Citrus

Serves 4 / **Prep time:** 10 minutes / **Cook time:** 20 minutes

There's something about the aroma of cumin, beans, and citrus cooking together that's so incredibly mouthwatering. The spices lend depth to this super-easy soup, striking a balance between spicy, savory, sweet, and sour. This is the kind of soup that begs to be served with a hefty slice of Jalapeño Corn Bread with Honey Butter (page 131) and topped with fresh cilantro.

3 tablespoons olive oil

1 white or yellow
  onion, chopped

1 red bell pepper, chopped

2 celery stalks, chopped

6 garlic cloves, chopped

2 teaspoons ground cumin

1 teaspoon chili powder

1 teaspoon salt

2 (15-ounce) cans
  black beans, drained
  and rinsed

2 cups water

Grated zest and juice of
  1 orange

Juice of 2 limes

Chopped fresh cilantro, for
  garnish (optional)

1. **Sauté the vegetables.** Heat a Dutch oven over medium heat. Add the olive oil, onion, bell pepper, and celery. Cook for about 7 minutes, stirring occasionally. Add the garlic, cumin, chili powder, and salt. Stir to coat the vegetables and turn off the heat to avoid burning.

2. **Simmer the beans.** Add the black beans and water. Using a spatula, stir to combine, scraping along the bottom of the pot to release any browned bits. Bring the soup to a simmer over medium heat and cook for 8 minutes.

3. **Season and serve.** Stir in the orange zest, orange juice, and lime juice to taste. (Salt and acid lift the savory flavors of this soup.) Garnish with cilantro (if using). Refrigerate leftovers for up to 2 days.

Turmeric Vegetable Soup

Serves 6 / **Prep time:** 10 minutes / **Cook time:** 20 minutes

I like to call this my immunity-boosting soup because the spices stimulate the immune system and turmeric is known for its anti-inflammatory properties. Turmeric has an earthy, ginger-like flavor and a deep orange color that melds perfectly with the sweet potato, poblano peppers, and corn. The coconut broth is soothing, healthy, and delicious.

2 tablespoons olive oil

1 sweet potato, peeled and diced

1 teaspoon salt, plus more for seasoning

5 garlic cloves, minced

1 poblano chile, seeded and chopped

2 cups frozen corn

1 tablespoon chili powder

1 teaspoon ground cumin

1 teaspoon ground turmeric

½ cup dry white wine

4 cups water

1 (14-ounce) can coconut milk

1. **Sauté the vegetables.** In a Dutch oven over medium heat, warm the olive oil. Add the sweet potato and salt. Stir to combine and cook for 7 minutes or until the potato begins to brown. Stir in the garlic, poblano, and corn. Cook for 3 minutes more.

2. **Deglaze and simmer.** Add the chili powder, cumin, and turmeric, and toss to coat the vegetables. Cook for 1 minute. Stir in the white wine and deglaze the pot, scraping along the bottom of the pot to release any browned bits. Add the water and increase the heat to medium-high. Bring the soup to a simmer and cook for about 5 minutes, until heated through.

3. **Season and serve.** Turn off the heat and stir in the coconut milk. Taste and, if the soup is bland, season with salt. Refrigerate leftovers for up to 3 days.

SERVING TIP: Since turmeric gives this soup such an earthy flavor, I recommend serving it with a floral garnish such as chopped fresh cilantro. Add delicate herbs at the last moment to maximize their aromatic properties.

Chicken and Rice Soup

Serves 6 / **Prep time:** 10 minutes / **Cook time:** 30 minutes

Stretch a rotisserie chicken even further by adding it to soup with rice. Normally, cooking rice requires a precise amount of liquid, but there's nothing fussy about adding rice to soup because there's plenty of liquid to cover the grain's expansion. For an even richer flavor, add a splash of cream or 1 cup of evaporated milk.

1 leek

1 tablespoon olive oil

2 garlic cloves, minced

6 thyme sprigs

1 bay leaf

8 cups chicken stock

½ cup long-grain
 white rice

Salt

2 cups shredded
 rotisserie chicken

2 cups frozen
 mixed vegetables

Freshly ground
 black pepper

Fresh parsley, for
 garnish (optional)

1. **Chop and sweat the vegetables.** Remove the leek's tough outer green portions. Cut lengthwise down the center of the leek's white stalk, but keep the root end intact. Fan the leek under running water to wash away any sand. Thinly slice the leek and discard the root. In a Dutch oven over medium heat, warm the olive oil. Add the leek and sweat it for 4 minutes, until soft. Add the garlic and cook, stirring occasionally, for 2 minutes.

2. **Add the liquid and simmer the rice.** Add the thyme, bay leaf, chicken stock, rice, and a pinch of salt. Stir, then cover the pot and simmer for 15 minutes or until the rice is tender.

3. **Add the chicken and vegetables.** Add the chicken and frozen vegetables. Simmer for 3 minutes. Taste and adjust the seasoning with salt and pepper as desired. Remove the bay leaf. Garnish with parsley (if using). Refrigerate leftovers for up to 3 days.

INGREDIENT TIP: People often wonder what the difference is between broth and stock. The answer is salt. Stock is completely unsalted, and broth is good enough to drink by itself because it's a seasoned stock. If you use broth instead of stock, omit the salt in step 2 and season to taste once the soup is finished cooking.

French Onion Soup

Serves 6 / Prep time: 15 minutes / Cook time: 45 minutes

In culinary school, when my classmates and I would caramelize onions, we'd often finish at different times. Heat, moisture, and fat all affect the rate of caramelization, so it's best to follow a few guidelines rather than time the procedure. Coat the onions thoroughly in fat. Use salt to suck moisture out and encourage the sugars to come to the onion's surface. If you smell burning, quickly add a splash of water to keep the onions moist and lower the heat a bit.

8 tablespoons (1 stick)
  unsalted butter

4 white onions,
  thinly sliced

1 teaspoon salt, plus more
  for seasoning

2 garlic cloves, minced

3 tablespoons
  all-purpose flour

1 cup dry red wine

2 bay leaves

1 teaspoon freshly ground
  black pepper, plus more
  for seasoning

1 teaspoon dried thyme

8 cups beef stock

4 cups grated
  Gruyère cheese

Fresh parsley, for
  garnish (optional)

1. **Caramelize the onions.** Warm a Dutch oven over medium heat. Add the butter, onions, and salt. Stir and cook for about 20 minutes, monitoring the onions closely, until they are mushy, brown, and have a sweet taste.

2. **Add the flour and wine.** Turn the heat to medium-low. Add the garlic. Cook, stirring, for 1 minute. Stir in the flour and cook with the onions for at least 3 minutes, then add the red wine. Cook for about 1 minute, stirring to scrape up any browned bits from the bottom of the pot, until the wine has reduced by half.

3. **Add the beef stock and simmer.** Add the bay leaves, pepper, and thyme. Raise the heat to medium-high and add the beef stock. Simmer for 10 minutes. Using tongs, remove the bay leaves. Taste and season with more salt and pepper as desired.

4. **Preheat the broiler and melt the cheese.** When you're ready to serve, position an oven rack under the broiler so the Dutch oven will fit. Top the soup with a thick layer of the cheese, then broil for about 3 minutes or until the cheese is bubbly and golden brown. Ladle the soup with the cheese topping into bowls, and serve with crusty bread for dunking, if desired. Garnish with parsley (if using). Refrigerate leftovers for up to 4 days. To reheat the soup in the Dutch oven, simmer it over medium heat for about 5 minutes to melt the cheese and warm the soup.

Bone Broth Beef Stew

Serves 6 / **Prep time:** 15 minutes / **Cook time:** 2 hours 45 minutes

This classic beef stew is the ultimate cold weather comfort, with tender beef and vegetables enveloped in a savory bone broth. When stewing, it's good practice to season throughout the cooking process so the ingredients have plenty of time to develop and morph into something complex. At first glance, there are a lot of ingredients here, but most of them are pantry staples you may already have.

3 pounds boneless beef
   chuck, cut into bite-size
   cubes and patted dry
Salt
Freshly ground
   black pepper
3 tablespoons olive oil
2 white or yellow
   onions, chopped
¼ cup water (optional)
4 garlic cloves, minced
1½ tablespoons
   tomato paste
3 tablespoons
   all-purpose flour
2 cups dry red wine
2 cups beef bone broth
2 teaspoons
   Italian seasoning
1 pound small white
   potatoes (such as
   baby Yukons), peeled
   and chopped
4 carrots, chopped
Fresh parsley, for
   garnish (optional)

1. **Brown the beef.** Season the beef well with salt and pepper. In a Dutch oven over medium heat, warm the olive oil. Working in two batches to avoid overcrowding the pot, cook the beef for 5 to 10 minutes per side. Allow the beef several minutes of contact with the heat to develop a brown crust before turning it. Once the meat is evenly browned, use tongs to transfer it to a large bowl to retain the juices.

2. **Add the onions, garlic, tomato paste, and flour.** Add the onions to the Dutch oven and cook for about 6 minutes, stirring and scraping along the bottom of the pot with a wooden spoon to loosen any browned bits, until soft. If the onion appears dry, add the water. Stir in the garlic and tomato paste and return the beef with its juices to the pot, along with the flour. Stir well and cook for 2 minutes.

3. **Add the wet ingredients.** Stir in the red wine, bone broth, and Italian seasoning, scraping along the bottom of the pot to loosen any caramelized food. Cover the pot, reduce the heat to low, and simmer for 1 hour and 30 minutes.

4. **Add the potatoes and carrots.** Add the potatoes, the carrots, and a pinch each of salt and pepper to the pot. Re-cover the pot and simmer the stew for 45 minutes more. Serve the stew garnished with parsley (if using) and crusty bread, if desired. Refrigerate leftovers, which taste even better the next day, for up to 4 days.

Chicken Pozole Verde

Serves 6 / **Prep time:** 10 minutes / **Cook time:** 15 minutes

Pozole is an exemplary Mexican stew, featuring hominy and chiles in an invigorating stock. Hominy has a gentle, grain-like taste that's distinctly savory and chewy. What makes the stock green is a combination of blended serrano chiles, tomatillos, and fresh cilantro. Tomatillos, which look like green tomatoes covered with papery husks, can be found in the produce section of most grocery stores. I like to serve this soup with a crunchy topping of cooling shredded cabbage to counteract the spiciness.

1 tablespoon olive oil

1 pound boneless, skinless chicken thighs, roughly chopped into bite-size pieces

1 teaspoon salt, plus more for seasoning

3 tomatillos, husked, rinsed, and roughly chopped

2 serrano chiles, seeded and roughly chopped

1 white onion, roughly chopped

2 teaspoons dried oregano

4 cups chicken stock

1 handful fresh cilantro

1 (29-ounce) can white hominy (no need to drain)

1. **Brown the chicken.** In a Dutch oven over medium heat, warm the oil. Season the chicken with a pinch of salt and add it to the pot. Cook, stirring occasionally, for 5 minutes, just until the chicken is browned on all sides. Transfer the chicken to a bowl and set aside.

2. **Simmer and blend the stock.** Combine the tomatillos, serranos, onion, oregano, salt, and chicken stock in the Dutch oven. Increase the heat to medium-high and simmer the soup for 5 minutes. Add the cilantro. Using an immersion blender, blend the soup on high speed until it is light green and smooth.

3. **Stew and serve.** Return the chicken and any juices to the pot and add the hominy. Simmer for 5 minutes. Refrigerate leftovers for up to 3 days.

TECHNICAL TIP: Instead of an immersion blender, use a slotted spoon to transfer the solid ingredients to a blender with 1 cup of the stock. Blend until smooth, then return the green stock to the Dutch oven.

Stewed Collard Greens with Beans and Ham

Serves 6 / **Prep time:** 10 minutes, plus overnight to soak the beans / **Cook time:** 1 hour

There's a tradition in my family to eat black-eyed peas on New Year's Day for good luck, but this soup tastes great all year long. When I can't find black-eyed peas, I use great northern beans because they are similar in size. If you're pressed for time, you can make this entire recipe in under 30 minutes with canned black-eyed peas, which are already cooked. Instead of 1 cup dried black-eyed peas, use at least two (15-ounce) cans to get about 3 cups of cooked beans.

1 cup dried
   black-eyed peas

4 bacon slices,
   roughly chopped

1 yellow onion, chopped

3 carrots, chopped

5 garlic cloves, chopped

2 cups chicken stock

2 cups chopped cooked
   ham, preferably smoked

3 cups water

1 bunch collard greens,
   rinsed and chopped

1 tablespoon apple
   cider vinegar

Salt

Freshly ground
   black pepper

1. **Soak the peas.** Place the black-eyed peas in a large bowl, then pour in enough water to cover them completely. Let soak overnight. Drain.

2. **Simmer the peas.** In a Dutch oven over medium heat, cook the bacon, stirring occasionally, for about 3 minutes or until browned. Add the onion, carrots, and garlic. Cook for 5 minutes or until tender. Add the chicken stock, ham, drained black-eyed peas, and water. Cover the pot and simmer for 50 minutes, stirring occasionally.

3. **Stir in the greens.** Add the collard greens and vinegar to the pot. Stir to wilt the greens. Taste and season with salt and pepper. Test several peas to make sure they are tender and fully cooked, then ladle the soup into bowls to serve. Refrigerate leftovers for up to 3 days.

TECHNICAL TIP: If you forget to soak the peas, place them in a large pot full of water over high heat. When the water boils, turn off the heat and let the peas sit for 1 hour in the hot water. Black-eyed peas typically take 45 minutes to cook, but if they are old, they may require more time.

'd's Pie

ie: 15 minutes / **Cook time:** 35 minutes

ful pie, I like to stew the vegetables in the beef's juices. Mashed
d thyme are my favorite flavor combo, but I've seen variants that
add chili powder or corn to the beef, or top the potatoes with cheddar cheese. Whatever your preferred flavors may be, the secret to getting perfectly fluffy, lump-free
mashed potatoes is to use a ricer.

1 teaspoon salt, plus more
 for seasoning

3 russet potatoes, peeled
 and chopped

½ teaspoon freshly ground
 black pepper, plus more
 for seasoning

2 tablespoons olive
 oil, divided

1 yellow onion,
 roughly chopped

1 carrot, roughly chopped

3 garlic cloves,
 roughly chopped

1½ pounds ground beef

1 cup frozen peas

2 tablespoons ketchup

2 teaspoons dried thyme

1. **Preheat the oven.** Preheat the oven to 350°F.

2. **Boil the potatoes.** Fill a Dutch oven halfway
   with water and season with a large pinch of salt.
   Bring the water to a boil over high heat. Add the
   potatoes, return the water to a boil, and cook
   for about 6 minutes or until the potatoes are
   fork-tender. Place a colander in the sink and
   drain the potatoes. Then, transfer the potatoes to
   a bowl and mash them, preferably with a ricer.
   Season with salt and pepper and set aside.

3. **Sauté the vegetables.** In the Dutch oven over
   medium heat, heat 1 tablespoon of olive oil. Add
   the onion, carrot, and garlic. Cook for 5 minutes,
   stirring occasionally, until the vegetables begin to
   soften. Stir in the salt and pepper.

4. **Cook the beef.** Scoop the vegetables into a pile on one side of the Dutch oven to clear a space for the beef. Add the ground beef and cook, stirring to break up the meat, for 5 minutes or until the meat is browned and no pink remains. (It does not need to be crispy.) Stir in the peas, ketchup, and thyme.

5. **Bake the casserole.** Spread the beef mixture into an even layer, then top it with a smooth layer of mashed potatoes. Drizzle the top with the remaining 1 tablespoon of olive oil. Transfer the Dutch oven to the oven and bake for 15 minutes. Serve scoops of stewed beef with the potatoes on top. Refrigerate leftovers for up to 4 days.

MAKE IT CONTEMPORARY: Add corn, chopped chiles, and cheese to the mix, or use a combination of ground lamb and rosemary with a mashed sweet potato topping for a spin on the classic savory profile.

ROAST WHOLE CHICKEN OVER RADISHES, page 82

Braises and Roasts

CHAPTER FIVE

A moist and tender pot roast is the iconic Dutch oven dish, with large chunks of meat swimming in rich gravy. Although the Dutch oven is uniquely designed to keep food moist, it might surprise you to learn how well the Dutch oven achieves crispy textures, too. Interestingly, you can often achieve both tender and crispy textures in the same dish by mindfully positioning the food within the pot. Take the Roast Whole Chicken over Radishes (page 82), for example, which gets a crispy, golden skin in the oven while the radishes collect the moist drippings underneath.

Buffalo Chicken Wings

Serves 4 / Prep time: 15 minutes / Cook time: 1 hour

For years, I'd been testing different chicken wing recipes, but I never quite landed on "the one." This Dutch oven version is it. The baking powder keeps the outsides of the wings dry. Then, for that finger-lickin'-good experience, you just roll the roasted wings in a tangy, spicy buffalo sauce (I prefer Frank's RedHot because it's acidic and fairly mild). Make sure to use parchment paper to prevent the chicken skin from sticking to the bottom of your Dutch oven.

2 pounds bone-in, skin-on chicken wingettes

2½ teaspoons baking powder

½ teaspoon salt, plus more for seasoning

¼ teaspoon garlic powder

3 tablespoons unsalted butter

½ teaspoon honey

⅓ cup hot sauce, such as Frank's RedHot

1. **Preheat the oven.** Preheat the oven to 425°F. Line the Dutch oven with parchment paper.

2. **Dry and coat the wings.** Pat the chicken wings dry with a paper towel, then arrange them in a single layer in the prepared Dutch oven. In a small bowl, stir together the baking powder, salt, and garlic powder. Sprinkle the seasoning over the wings, turning to coat both sides evenly.

3. **Roast.** Transfer the Dutch oven to the middle rack of the oven; roast the wings for 55 minutes or until golden and crispy. Remove from the oven and sprinkle with a pinch of salt.

4. **Toss the wings with sauce.** Transfer the wings to a serving platter. Remove the parchment paper from the still-hot Dutch oven, place the butter and honey inside, and let the residual heat of the Dutch oven melt the two ingredients together. Stir in the hot sauce just until the sauce is smooth. Pour the hot sauce over the wings and serve immediately. Refrigerate leftovers for up to 3 days.

Layered Roasted Ratatouille

Serves 6 / **Prep time:** 20 minutes / **Cook time:** 50 minutes

Ratatouille is a classic Provençal stew. I never quite liked the texture—until I discovered that roasting changes the texture and intensifies the flavor in a way I like. For this colorful version, slice the vegetables and stuff them sideways in a Dutch oven. About an hour later, you have a tender, juicy side dish or main course.

5 zucchini

1 eggplant

1 yellow bell pepper

1 red bell pepper

1 red onion

2 large red tomatoes, such as heirloom or beefsteak

6 garlic cloves

½ cup olive oil

3½ teaspoons salt

2 teaspoons dried oregano

1½ teaspoons freshly ground black pepper

¼ cup fresh basil leaves

1. **Preheat the oven.** Preheat the oven to 450°F.

2. **Cut the vegetables.** Thinly slice the zucchini, eggplant, bell peppers, red onion, and tomatoes. Transfer to a large bowl. Mince the garlic and add it to the bowl with the vegetables. Add the olive oil, salt, oregano, and pepper. Toss to coat.

3. **Layer and roast the vegetables.** Stack and arrange the vegetables in alternating layers, following the shape of your Dutch oven and stuffing them in sideways. Roast for 50 minutes, uncovered, until the vegetables release their juices and begin to brown. Remove the Dutch oven from the oven.

4. **Garnish and serve.** Stack the basil leaves, roll them into a cigar shape, and slice thinly across the roll to make thin ribbons. Sprinkle the basil over the vegetables and serve hot. Ratatouille makes excellent leftovers. Refrigerate in the Dutch oven to portion and reheat easily for up to 4 days.

MAKE-AHEAD TIP: Make this recipe in advance, and cook or reheat it when ready. I like to serve it family style and let people spoon it over Parmesan Polenta with Thyme-Roasted Mushrooms (page 42).

Pork Tenderloin with Roasted Fennel

Serves 4 / **Prep time:** 10 minutes / **Cook time:** 20 minutes

A pork tenderloin roast makes a quick and easy lean protein dinner. Fresh fennel adds moisture and a slight anise flavor to the pork as the fennel cooks beneath it. Note that the recommended temperature for pork is 145°F, which will be pink inside. If you want to cook the pork longer, it will not dry out if you take it to 150°F.

1 fennel bulb

1 pound pork tenderloin

2 teaspoons olive oil

1 teaspoon salt

1 teaspoon freshly ground
   black pepper

1 teaspoon Dijon mustard

½ teaspoon fennel seeds

1 teaspoon apple
   cider vinegar

1. **Preheat the oven.** Preheat the oven to 450°F.

2. **Cut the fennel.** Remove the stalks of the fennel bulb and reserve the fennel fronds for garnish. Cut the white fennel bulb into large 2-inch-thick slices. Spread the fennel in a single layer in a Dutch oven.

3. **Roast the pork tenderloin.** Place the pork tenderloin on top of the fennel. Season it all over with the olive oil, salt, pepper, Dijon, and fennel seeds. Transfer the pot to the oven and roast for 15 minutes or until the spices have darkened and you can see bits of caramelization. Remove from the oven and let it rest for 5 minutes.

4. **Finish and serve.** Transfer the pork to a cutting board and slice it into thick medallions. Pour the vinegar over the fennel and stir, scraping up any browned bits from the bottom of the pot. Serve each serving of pork with some roasted fennel and a bit of pan jus. Refrigerate leftovers for up to 3 days.

INGREDIENT TIP: Most grocery stores sell pork tenderloin already trimmed, with the silver skin removed. If you see a tough, shimmery skin, remove it with a sharp knife before seasoning.

Cheese Enchiladas in Red Sauce

Serves 4 / Prep time: 10 minutes / Cook time: 25 minutes

I'm from the Southwest, so my idea of comfort food is cheesy enchiladas, and you'd better believe these Dutch oven enchiladas are ooey gooey and swimming in a magical chile sauce. In terms of heat, it's on the mild side. I like to serve these enchiladas Arizona style—with a mound of finely shredded cold lettuce—but you could also serve them with avocado slices and sliced scallions.

3 tablespoons
vegetable oil

8 corn tortillas

¼ cup chili powder

1 tablespoon ground cumin

1 teaspoon garlic powder

½ teaspoon dried oregano

1 (15-ounce) can
tomato sauce

1½ cups vegetable stock

2 teaspoons cornstarch

1 teaspoon salt

4 cups shredded cheddar
Jack cheese (14 ounces)

1. **Preheat the oven.** Position a rack in the center of the oven and preheat the oven to 400°F.

2. **Soften the tortillas.** Preheat the Dutch oven over medium heat. Add the vegetable oil and pan-fry the tortillas for 20 seconds per side to soften them. Using tongs, transfer the tortillas to a paper towel–lined plate to drain. Turn off the heat.

3. **Make the red sauce.** While the Dutch oven cools, in a small bowl, stir together the chili powder, cumin, garlic powder, and oregano. Pour the spices into the pot, and let the pot's residual heat toast the spices for about 30 seconds, until they are aromatic. Add the tomato sauce, vegetable stock, cornstarch, and salt. Stir well, then turn the heat to medium. Bring the sauce to a simmer and cook, stirring, for 3 minutes to thicken.

4. **Braise the enchiladas.** Tuck some cheese inside each tortilla and roll it up. Place the rolled tortillas seam-side down in the red sauce. Using a spoon, cover the tortillas with the red sauce, then top with the remaining cheese. Transfer to the oven and bake for 15 minutes or until the cheese is completely melted. Serve with your favorite garnish. Refrigerate leftovers for up to 3 days.

INGREDIENT TIP: Use any Mexican-style cheese blend, or create your own with a combination of cheddar and Monterey Jack cheeses.

Honey Garlic–Glazed Shrimp and Broccoli

Serves 4 / **Prep time:** 15 minutes / **Cook time:** 10 minutes

This recipe is a good example of how a marinade can become a braising liquid or a finishing sauce. I like to remove the shrimp from the marinade and pan-fry them in oil to caramelize some of the sugars and then use the same marinade to cook the broccoli and finish the dish. Pan-searing the shrimp achieves a coating that locks in flavor. Buy frozen shrimp with tails on or off, and thaw them before cooking.

4 garlic cloves, minced

¼ cup honey

¼ cup tamari

2 pounds fresh shrimp, peeled and deveined

1 large head broccoli

1 tablespoon refined coconut oil

Chopped scallion, for garnish (optional)

1. **Marinate the shrimp.** In a large bowl, stir together the garlic, honey, tamari, and shrimp to coat. Set aside to marinate for 10 minutes. Meanwhile, cut the broccoli into bite-size pieces and set aside.

2. **Caramelize the shrimp.** In a Dutch oven over medium heat, heat the coconut oil. Working in batches, using tongs, remove the shrimp from the marinade and arrange them in a single layer in the pot, reserving the marinade. Cook the shrimp for about 3 minutes total, turning them halfway through so they are pink and caramelized on both sides. Transfer the cooked shrimp to a plate, then repeat with the remaining shrimp.

3. **Boil the marinade and cook the broccoli.** Return the cooked shrimp to the Dutch oven and add the reserved marinade and the broccoli. Braise, stirring, for 1 minute, just until the broccoli is bright green and cooked.

4. **Serve.** Serve the shrimp with the broccoli and pan sauce. Garnish with scallions (if using). Refrigerate leftovers for up to 2 days.

MAKE IT CONTEMPORARY: Add chopped, peeled fresh ginger and red pepper flakes to the marinade, and sear the shrimp in sesame oil.

Juicy Shredded Chicken Tinga

Serves 4 / **Prep time:** 10 minutes / **Cook time:** 1 hour

I like to use chicken thighs for this simple dish because the meat stays juicier and has more flavor than chicken breasts do. Once shredded, you just immerse the chicken in a simple tomato sauce with some spicy, smoky flavor from a canned chipotle pepper. Use one pepper for a mildly spicy tinga, or use two for a little more bang.

1 tablespoon olive oil

4 boneless, skinless chicken thighs

1 teaspoon salt

2 garlic cloves, chopped

1 canned chipotle pepper in adobo sauce, chopped

1 teaspoon dried oregano

½ teaspoon ground cumin

¾ cup canned fire-roasted crushed tomatoes

⅓ cup chicken stock

1. **Preheat the oven.** Position a rack in the center of the oven and preheat the oven to 400°F.

2. **Roast the chicken.** Spread the olive oil in the bottom of a Dutch oven and set the chicken thighs on top, turning to coat them in the oil. Season both sides with salt. Roast for 40 minutes.

3. **Shred and braise the chicken.** Let the chicken cool, then use your hands to tear the chicken into strips in the pot. Add the garlic and chipotle pepper to the Dutch oven along with the oregano, cumin, tomatoes with their juices, and chicken stock. Braise in the oven for 20 minutes. Serve the chicken tinga over rice, or use it as a filling for tacos. Refrigerate leftovers for up to 3 days.

INGREDIENT TIP: Short on time? Shred a rotisserie chicken and braise the meat in the chipotle tomato sauce (step 3) for a 30-minute meal.

Salt-Cured Crispy Pork Belly

Serves 6 / **Prep time:** 5 minutes, plus overnight to cure /
Cook time: 1 hour 55 minutes, plus 30 minutes to rest

A beautiful pork belly roast is forgiving to cook and yields tasty, juicy meat. Standard pork bellies are sold flat by the pound, but you can ask a butcher to roll and tie the pork so it holds its shape during cooking. I like to begin the roast at a lower temperature to render the fat and then finish at a high temperature to get those crispy cracklings that just about everybody loves.

2 pounds pork belly

3 tablespoons salt

1 tablespoon freshly
  ground black pepper

1. **Cure the pork.** Place the pork belly in a Dutch oven. Season generously with salt and pepper to create a thin layer all over the meat. Refrigerate, uncovered, overnight.

2. **Roast and slice the pork.** Position a rack in the center of the oven and preheat the oven to 275°F. Brush excess salt off the pork and pour any juices out of the pot. Bake for 1 hour and 30 minutes. Increase the oven temperature to 450°F and roast for about 25 minutes more, until the meat is golden brown. Remove the pot from the oven and let it rest for 30 minutes. Using tongs, transfer the pork to a cutting board. Slice and serve. Refrigerate leftovers for up to 3 days.

Apple Cider and Dijon–Glazed Pork Chops

Serves 6 / **Prep time:** 10 minutes / **Cook time:** 20 minutes

The combination of pork and apples always reminds me of fall and cloudy, unfiltered apple cider from just-pressed apples. It's a fun ingredient to work with because you can boil it down to a sticky glaze that pairs perfectly with pork's sweetness. For a meal, serve it with a side of roasted Brussels sprouts or any cooked bitter green.

1 tablespoon
  unsalted butter
6 (6-ounce) center-cut
  pork chops
1 teaspoon salt
½ teaspoon freshly ground
  black pepper
3 garlic cloves, minced
2 tablespoons apple
  cider vinegar
2 cups apple cider
1 teaspoon Dijon mustard
1 rosemary sprig, leaves
  removed and minced

1. **Preheat the oven.** Preheat the oven to 450°F.

2. **Season and sear the pork.** In a Dutch oven over medium heat, melt the butter. Season the pork chops all over with the salt and pepper, then add to the pot. Fry for 6 to 7 minutes per side, until browned, turning with tongs. Transfer the pork to a plate.

3. **Make the sauce.** Add the garlic to the Dutch oven, still over medium heat. Sauté, stirring, for 30 seconds. Stir in the vinegar, scraping along the bottom to release any browned bits, then add the cider and Dijon. Increase the heat to medium-high. Stir and bring to a simmer. Cook for about 5 minutes or until the sauce reduces and thickens.

4. **Braise the pork.** Add the rosemary to the glaze and return the pork chops to the sauce, turning to coat. Reheat the pork chops for 1 minute, then serve with the sauce. Refrigerate leftovers for up to 4 days.

INGREDIENT TIP: Pork chops go by several different labels. If you don't see "pork chops," look for "pork loin." You want roughly 1-inch-thick slices, but any thickness will work if you have a meat thermometer. The pork is done when it reaches an internal temperature of 145°F.

Roast Whole Chicken over Radishes

Serves 4 / Prep time: 15 minutes / Cook time: 1 hour 15 minutes, plus 15 minutes to rest

I would own a Dutch oven just so I could roast whole chickens. This recipe is especially vibrant, with peppery radishes absorbing the savory drippings of the chicken. It's an elegant and earthy spring dinner that's easy to make yet impressive enough for company. I like to wilt the leaves of the radishes in the pan juices just before serving because they take on tons of flavor and provide the perfect bitter contrast.

2 bunches whole radishes

3 tablespoons olive oil, divided

Salt

1 (4- to 4½-pound) whole chicken

Freshly ground black pepper

3 scallions, rinsed, roots trimmed off

1 lemon, quartered

1. **Prepare the radishes.** Preheat the oven to 425°F. Wash and trim the radish greens and set them aside for later. Halve the radish roots lengthwise and spread them out in a Dutch oven. Toss with 1 tablespoon of olive oil and a pinch of salt.

2. **Season and stuff the chicken.** Pat the chicken dry with paper towels, then brush it all over with the remaining 2 tablespoons of olive oil. Season the entire chicken with salt and pepper, and place it on top of the radishes in the Dutch oven. Fold the scallions and stuff them and the lemon inside the chicken's cavity.

3. **Roast and serve the chicken.** Roast the chicken, uncovered, for 1 hour and 15 minutes or until the juices run clear and an instant read thermometer reads 165°F when inserted into the thickest part of a breast. Remove the pot from the oven. While the chicken is hot, stuff the reserved radish greens in the pot around the chicken to steam; let rest for 15 minutes. Transfer the chicken to a cutting board. Carve and serve it with the wilted radish greens, pan juices, and roasted radishes.

White Wine and Caper–Braised Chicken Thighs

Serves 4 / **Prep time:** 10 minutes / **Cook time:** 25 minutes

This dish will remind you of lemony chicken piccata, but instead of pounded and breaded chicken breasts, this recipe uses the heating power of the Dutch oven to crisp the chicken's skin, eliminating the need for any breading. Chicken thighs are a great choice for Dutch oven cooking because they stay tender and juicy. For an alcohol-free meal, replace the white wine with 1 tablespoon caper juice or white wine vinegar.

FOR THE CHICKEN

4 skin-on chicken thighs (about 2 pounds total)

Salt

Freshly ground black pepper

2 tablespoons olive oil

FOR THE SAUCE

2 tablespoons capers, drained

½ cup chicken stock

¼ cup dry white wine

Juice of 1 lemon

2 tablespoons unsalted butter

¼ cup fresh parsley, chopped

1. **Preheat the oven.** Preheat the oven to 450°F.

2. **Dry the chicken.** Pat the chicken dry with a paper towel. Season both sides with salt and pepper.

3. **Sear skin-side down.** Warm a Dutch oven over medium heat. Add the olive oil and place the chicken, skin-side down, in the hot oil (it should sizzle). Cook for at least 5 minutes to blister the skin.

4. **Roast the chicken.** Using tongs, turn the chicken thighs. Roast in the oven, uncovered, for 15 minutes. Using tongs, transfer the chicken to a cutting board.

5. **Make the sauce and serve.** In the still-warm Dutch oven, stir together the capers, chicken stock, white wine, lemon juice, and butter. Use the residual heat of the pot to melt the butter. Sprinkle the parsley over the sauce. Add the chicken thighs to the sauce, skin-side up, and bring the sauce to a simmer over medium heat. Cook for 1 minute. Spoon the caper sauce over the chicken just before serving to keep some of the crispy texture of the skin. Refrigerate leftovers for up to 3 days.

Hoisin Meatballs

Serves 6 / **Prep time:** 10 minutes / **Cook time:** 15 minutes

Hoisin is a thick, fragrant sauce that adds a sweet and salty layer to these pork and beef meatballs. I've found that you get more tender meatballs if you mix them lightly for less than a minute. To form the meatballs, I use an ice cream scoop to get equal portions and then smooth and reshape them with my palms.

Olive oil, for preparing the
   Dutch oven
1 small yellow onion
3 garlic cloves
1 (2-inch) piece fresh
   ginger, peeled
1 pound ground beef
1 pound ground pork
2 large eggs
¾ cup plain bread crumbs
1 teaspoon salt
½ teaspoon red
   pepper flakes
1 cup hoisin sauce

1. **Preheat the oven.** Preheat the oven to 425°F. Brush the bottom of a Dutch oven with a thin layer of olive oil.

2. **Mince the onion, garlic, and ginger.** Halve the onion and mince it. Measure ¼ cup minced onion and place it in a large bowl (reserve the rest of the onion for another use). Mince the garlic and ginger and add them to the bowl.

3. **Mix and form the meatballs.** Add the ground beef, ground pork, eggs, bread crumbs, salt, and red pepper flakes to the bowl. Mix the ingredients by hand just until combined. Form 12 smooth meatballs and set them inside the Dutch oven. Roast, uncovered, for 10 minutes.

4. **Bake with hoisin sauce.** Spoon the hoisin sauce over the meatballs and bake for 5 minutes more. Serve the meatballs over rice, if desired. Refrigerate leftovers for up to 4 days.

MAKE IT CLASSIC: Instead of ginger and hoisin, season the meat with Italian seasoning and grated Parmesan cheese, then serve with marinara sauce.

Kimchi Pot Roast Beef

Serves 4 / **Prep time:** 2 minutes / **Cook time:** 2 hours 30 minutes

This simple, bold kimchi beef is a mouthwatering experience. You slowly roast the beef with a little braising action from the kimchi so those rich, tangy flavors meld. I love how the kimchi moderates the beef's richness while keeping the beef really tender and moist.

2 pounds cubed beef stew meat, preferably well marbled

1 teaspoon salt

1 teaspoon freshly ground black pepper

2½ cups Korean kimchi, with juices

1. **Preheat the oven.** Position a rack in the center of the oven and preheat the oven to 275°F.

2. **Prepare and roast the beef.** Place the beef in a Dutch oven and season it all over with salt and pepper. Pour the kimchi over the beef and stir to distribute. Roast, uncovered, for 2 hours.

3. **Check the roast and serve.** Stir, cover the pot, and roast for 30 minutes more. Serve as-is or ladled over steamed rice. Refrigerate leftovers for up to 4 days.

SUBSTITUTION TIP: You can absolutely use this recipe with other cuts of beef. Specifically, look for fatty, well-marbled cuts such as short ribs, spare ribs, or beef chuck roast.

Mojo-Marinated Roasted Pork

Serves 6 / **Prep time:** 15 minutes, plus overnight to marinate /
Cook time: 2 hours, plus 30 minutes to rest

When it comes to pork, no sandwich can compete with the almighty Cubano: a crunchy pressed sandwich stuffed with melted Swiss, ham, Dijon, mayonnaise, and pickles (see tip). Instead of deli ham, though, I marinate pork in a tart, herbaceous sauce to give it even more character. This pork has such a savory-yet-fresh flavor from mint and cilantro, and you get an unexpected pop of sweet and sour from the orange and lime.

8 garlic cloves

¼ cup fresh oregano leaves, or 1 tablespoon dried oregano

1 bunch fresh cilantro

½ cup fresh mint leaves

Grated zest and juice of 2 oranges

Juice of 4 limes

2 teaspoons ground cumin

1 tablespoon salt, plus more for seasoning

1 tablespoon freshly ground black pepper, plus more for seasoning

½ cup olive oil

1 (3½-pound) boneless pork shoulder

1. **Make the mojo marinade.** Smash the garlic and mince the oregano, cilantro, and mint, and combine them in a Dutch oven. Stir in the orange zest, orange juice, lime juice, cumin, salt, pepper, and olive oil.

2. **Score the pork.** Using a sharp knife, score a crosshatch pattern around the outside of the pork ¼ inch deep. Place the pork in the Dutch oven and turn it to coat with the marinade, stuffing the smashed garlic into the crevices. Cover and refrigerate overnight.

3. **Roast the pork.** Preheat the oven to 375°F. Discard the marinade and season the pork all over with salt and pepper. Return the pork to the pot and roast for 1 hour. Turn the pork and roast for 1 hour more. The pork will have very dark brown caramelized pockets across the surface, especially where the herbs were sitting. Let rest for 30 minutes, then transfer to a cutting board. Slice and serve. Refrigerate leftovers for up to 4 days.

TECHNICAL TIP: Use the Dutch oven as a panini press to make mojo-marinated roasted pork paninis. Heat the Dutch oven over medium-high heat until hot. Make the sandwiches, filled with Swiss cheese, mojo-marinated roasted pork, Dijon mustard, mayonnaise, and pickles, and place them on a cutting board. Place the heated Dutch oven on top of the sandwiches to weigh them down and toast the bread. Let sit for 2 minutes. Flip the sandwiches and press again until the bread is golden, about 2 minutes more.

Tandoori Chicken

Serves 4 / **Prep time:** 15 minutes, plus overnight to marinate / **Cook time:** 25 minutes

I prefer to use dark meat for tandoori chicken, so it's a great way to experiment with chicken thighs. You don't need a tandoori oven to make this delicious chicken—just a Dutch oven and a spiced marinade. Try to find a thick plain yogurt, such as Greek yogurt, which will stick to the chicken and tenderize the meat.

1 cup plain Greek yogurt

1 tablespoon freshly
squeezed lime juice

2 teaspoons freshly
ground black pepper

2 teaspoons garam masala

1 teaspoon
ground turmeric

¼ teaspoon ground ginger

2 pounds bone-in
chicken thighs

Chopped fresh cilantro, for
garnish (optional)

1. **Marinate the chicken.** In a Dutch oven, stir together the yogurt, lime juice, pepper, garam masala, turmeric, and ginger. Using a sharp knife, make 3 incisions, ¼ inch deep, in each chicken thigh. Add the chicken to the marinade and rub the marinade all over the chicken. Cover the pot and refrigerate overnight.

2. **Roast the chicken.** Preheat the oven to 400°F. Roast the chicken in the marinade, uncovered, for about 25 minutes, until it begins to brown and is cooked through. To check if the chicken is done, pierce it with a knife; if the juices run clear, the meat is cooked. Some areas where there is marinade will be blackened a bit—this intense caramelization is what you want. Serve the chicken garnished with cilantro (if using) over rice, if desired. Refrigerate leftovers for up to 3 days.

Cuban Shredded Beef

Serves 6 / Prep time: 15 minutes / Cook time: 3 hours 45 minutes

Several years ago, during my first visit to Central America, I found myself appreciating the balance of starches, vegetables, and meat on every plate. I was especially drawn to a moist, flavorful dish called ropa vieja, *which is braised shredded beef soaking in a warm, briny tomato sauce. Every time I make this dish, it brings me back to Costa Rica, where they serve it with a side salad,* gallo pinto *(beans and rice), and plantains.*

1 white onion, chopped

3 garlic cloves, chopped

2 tablespoons tomato paste

2 tablespoons olive oil

2 teaspoons ground cumin

2 bay leaves

½ teaspoon salt, plus more for seasoning

1 cup beef stock

2½ pounds boneless beef chuck

¼ cup pitted green olives

3 tablespoons olive juice

1. **Preheat the oven.** Preheat the oven to 350°F.

2. **Set up the braising liquid.** In a Dutch oven over medium high heat, stir together the onion, garlic, tomato paste, olive oil, cumin, bay leaves, salt, and beef stock. Bring to a simmer and stir to create a sauce.

3. **Braise the beef.** Put the beef in the sauce and pour the olives and olive juice over the beef. Season with a pinch of salt. Place the lid on the pot and braise in the oven for 3 hours and 30 minutes or until the meat is tender enough to be shredded with a fork and the liquid has reduced.

4. **Shred the beef.** Remove and discard the bay leaves. Using 2 forks, shred the meat in the pot. Swirl it in the sauce and serve hot over rice, if desired. Refrigerate leftovers for up to 4 days.

MAKE IT CLASSIC: Instead of cumin and olives, use 2 teaspoons of garlic powder and 2 tablespoons of Worcestershire sauce.

Stout-Braised Pot Roast

Serves 6 / Prep time: 15 minutes / Cook time: 4 hours 15 minutes, plus 10 minutes to rest

It's hard to go wrong with beef pot roast, especially on a cold day. The stout adds a rich, full flavor to contrast the carrots' sweetness. The hardest part about this recipe is waiting patiently while the beef gets tender in the oven.

3 pounds boneless beef
   chuck roast

Salt

Freshly ground
   black pepper

2 tablespoons olive oil

3 tablespoons
   all-purpose flour

1½ cups stout beer

1 white onion,
   roughly chopped

1 celery stalk,
   roughly chopped

1 rosemary sprig, stem
   removed, minced

1 pound baby carrots

1 pound thin-skinned
   baby potatoes

1. **Preheat the oven.** Position a rack in the center of the oven and preheat the oven to 350°F.

2. **Brown the beef.** Trim any excess fat from the beef, and season it well all over with salt and pepper. In a Dutch oven over medium-high heat, heat the olive oil. Add the beef to the hot oil and cook for about 5 minutes per side, until browned. Transfer to a plate.

3. **Make a roux.** Reduce the heat to medium. Add the flour to the oil and cook, stirring frequently, for 5 minutes. Add the beer and stir to form a sauce.

4. **Add the vegetables and beef.** Place the beef in the center of the Dutch oven, and place the onion, celery, rosemary, baby carrots, and baby potatoes around the roast. Sprinkle the vegetables with salt and pepper.

5. **Roast and serve.** Transfer the Dutch oven to the oven and roast, uncovered, for 4 hours or until the meat is tender. Remove the pot from the oven. Use a spoon to skim off the clear layer of fat from the surface of the liquid. Transfer the roast to a cutting board and let it rest for 10 minutes. Using a sharp knife, cut the roast into thick slices; serve with the vegetables and gravy.

Spicy Eggplant Parmesan

Serves 4 / **Prep time:** 15 minutes / **Cook time:** 1 hour 5 minutes

Eggplant Parm lives and dies on how well the eggplant is cooked (if you've ever had undercooked eggplant, you know what I mean). Raw eggplant set in pasta sauce simply doesn't cook well, so the eggplant must be cooked before braising it in the liquid. Typically, the eggplant is fried, but that preparation can lead to an oily finished dish. I prefer to bake the breaded eggplant and then assemble the casserole layers. For the best flavor, use your favorite Italian marinara sauce.

3 eggplants, peeled and
 thinly sliced

2 teaspoons salt

2 large eggs

4 cups Italian-seasoned
 bread crumbs

1 (26-ounce) jar
 pasta sauce

1 pound shredded
 mozzarella cheese

⅓ cup grated Parmesan
 cheese, or more
 as desired

½ teaspoon red
 pepper flakes

Fresh basil leaves, for
 garnish (optional)

1. **Preheat the oven.** Preheat the oven to 350°F.

2. **Coat and bake the eggplant.** Collect the eggplant slices in a large bowl and sprinkle with the salt. In a medium bowl, whisk the eggs. Pour the bread crumbs onto a plate. One at a time, dip the eggplant slices into the egg, then into the bread crumbs, coating both sides. Create one single layer of breaded eggplant in the Dutch oven. Bake, uncovered, for 10 minutes. Transfer the baked eggplant to a plate and repeat with the remaining eggplant.

3. **Assemble the casserole.** Pour half the pasta sauce into the Dutch oven. Place a layer of eggplant slices on top, followed by a layer of mozzarella cheese. Sprinkle half the Parmesan over the mozzarella, and season with the red pepper flakes. Repeat with the remaining sauce, eggplant, and cheeses.

4. **Bake the casserole.** Bake for about 45 minutes, until bubbly and golden brown on top. Serve garnished with torn fresh basil leaves (if using). Refrigerate leftovers for up to 3 days.

Boeuf Bourguignon

Serves 6 / **Prep time:** 15 minutes / **Cook time:** 4 hours

This red wine–braised beef is the first dish I ever made in a Dutch oven, a turning point for me as a cook. So, while this is not a quick dish, it serves as a manual for how to use your Dutch oven to build deep flavor with simple ingredients. With this recipe as a base, you can include carrots, baby potatoes, and rosemary—and even a spoonful of tomato paste, if you wish.

3½ pounds boneless beef
   chuck roast, cut into
   2-inch cubes
Salt
Freshly ground
   black pepper
3 bacon slices
2 yellow onions, quartered
¼ cup water (optional)
8 ounces
   mushrooms, quartered
2 cups Malbec wine
4 cups beef stock
1 head garlic
2 bay leaves
6 thyme sprigs

1. **Preheat the oven.** Preheat the oven to 325°F.

2. **Brown the beef.** Season the beef all over with salt and pepper. In a Dutch oven over medium heat, cook the bacon for about 4 minutes, until crisp. Transfer the bacon to a large bowl, leaving the fat in the pot. Add the seasoned beef to the bacon fat. Sear for about 10 minutes, turning, until browned on all sides. Transfer the beef to the bowl with the bacon.

3. **Caramelize the onions and mushrooms.** Turn the heat to medium-low. Add the onions to the pot and sauté for about 10 minutes, until tender and brown, adding the water (if needed) to prevent burning. Using a slotted spoon, transfer the onions to the bowl with the meat. Spread the mushrooms out as much as possible in the pot and cook for 2 minutes without stirring. Return the beef, bacon, and onions to the pot.

4. **Add the liquids and aromatics.** Add the wine and beef stock. Halve the entire head of garlic horizontally; add both halves to the pot with the bay leaves and thyme.

5. **Braise in the oven.** Cover the Dutch oven and transfer it to the oven. Braise for about 3 hours and 30 minutes, until a fork pierces the meat easily. Transfer the meat and vegetables to a serving dish and skim off the fat from the surface of the liquid. Remove and discard the thyme, bay leaves, and garlic, and spoon the sauce over the beef and vegetables to serve. Refrigerate leftovers for up to 3 days.

TECHNICAL TIP: If you want a gravy consistency to the sauce, sprinkle 3 tablespoons of all-purpose flour over the mushrooms in step 3. Cook the mushrooms for 3 minutes, stirring, then proceed as written.

FRYBREAD NAVAJO TACOS, page 111

Fried Foods

CHAPTER SIX

Get ready for crispy bites and irresistibly rich flavors, because your Dutch oven is made for frying. I'll cover everything you need to know: batters, frying methods, quick sauces, and spice blends, too.

If you have a Dutch oven, there's no need to own a dedicated fryer. A Dutch oven is the perfect tool for both pan-frying and deep-frying small cuts of food quickly. A Dutch oven filled with oil takes a little time to warm, but, once there, a Dutch oven's mass excels at keeping the oil temperature constant, which is essential for achieving that satisfyingly crisp texture.

Each recipe in this chapter is equipped with safeguards to make frying manageable and fun. You can approach every recipe with or without a thermometer, since each includes the recommended temperature and helpful descriptions of how to tell when the oil might be too cold or too hot. I often refer to "testers"—using that first piece of food to indicate when to add the rest of the batch—a great work-around if you don't own a thermometer.

When frying, remember to avoid heating the oil to its smoking point; a good range for frying is between 350°F and 400°F. Because hot oil at these temperatures can cause burns, it's vital to rely on tools for moving food or oil in and out of the Dutch oven. Always let the oil cool completely before attempting to transfer it to a container, and never add water to hot oil!

Crispy White Fish with Garlic and Mint Sauce

Serves 4 / **Prep time:** 10 minutes / **Cook time:** 10 minutes

This dish is the epitome of fresh fish fast. Pan-frying in a bit of oil with a light flour dredge is a spectacular way to prepare any boneless white fish. What really makes this meal exceptional is the minty garlic sauce that comes together in about 3 minutes. After cooking the fish, sweat shallots and garlic in olive oil until soft and caramelized, then add a bit of vinegar to brighten the flavors and deglaze the Dutch oven.

¼ cup olive oil

¼ cup all-purpose flour

4 frozen tilapia
   fillets, thawed

Salt

Freshly ground
   black pepper

2 shallots, finely chopped

6 garlic cloves,
   roughly chopped

½ teaspoon red
   pepper flakes

1 bunch fresh mint,
   leaves chopped

1 tablespoon red
   wine vinegar

1. **Sear the fish.** In a Dutch oven over medium-high heat, heat the olive oil. Spread the flour on a plate. Season each fillet with salt and pepper, then press both sides into the flour, shaking to remove the excess. Cook the tilapia in the hot oil for about 2 minutes per side, until brown and crispy. Remove the fish from the pot, and set it aside on a serving platter.

2. **Make the sauce.** Add the shallots to the pot with a pinch of salt and cook for 2 minutes, stirring frequently. Add the garlic and red pepper flakes and cook for 1 minute more. Turn the heat off and stir in the mint and vinegar, scraping along the bottom of the pot to release any browned bits. Spoon the sauce over the fish and serve immediately.

Tempura Vegetables with Dipping Sauce

Serves 6 / **Prep time:** 10 minutes / **Cook time:** 30 minutes

With tempura, the fresher and colder the batter, the better. So, to ensure that the batter hydrates slowly, this batter sits over a bowl of ice. Start dipping the sweet potato slices first, about six pieces at a time. You want a thorough coating and a thorough draining. When food first hits oil, it bubbles as moisture from the food steams. When the bubbling stops, the food's surface dehydrates enough to develop that highly coveted crispy crust. All that golden goodness needs little more than a salty dipping sauce.

4 cups canola oil

1 large egg

1 cup cold sparkling water

½ cup vodka

1 cup white rice flour

½ teaspoon salt

2 sweet potatoes, peeled and cut into ⅛-inch-thick slices

1 head broccoli, cut into florets

¼ cup tamari

2 tablespoons rice vinegar

1 tablespoon mirin

1. **Heat the oil.** In a Dutch oven over medium heat, heat the canola oil to 375°F on a deep-fry thermometer.

2. **Make the batter.** Fill a large bowl with ice. Set a medium bowl over the ice and add the egg, sparkling water, and vodka. Whisk to combine. Whisk in the rice flour and salt; some lumps will remain.

3. **Dip and deep-fry the vegetables.** Line a large platter with paper towels. Set aside. Using tongs, dip the sweet potato slices, one at a time, into the batter to coat. Shake the slices over the bowl to allow excess batter to fall off, then, using tongs, transfer the sweet potato slices, *one at a time*, to the hot oil. Fry 6 pieces at a time for about 2 minutes per side until puffy and lightly golden brown, turning to ensure even cooking. Using a slotted spoon, transfer to the prepared platter to drain. Repeat with the broccoli florets, cooking them for about 3 minutes or until golden and crispy.

4. **Serve with dipping sauce.** In a small bowl, stir together the tamari, vinegar, and mirin. Serve as a dipping sauce with the vegetable tempura.

TECHNICAL TIP: If you don't have a thermometer, cook one slice of battered sweet potato; you want to see a lot of bubbling form around the tester right away, which will create a crunchy exterior that's not greasy. If the oil is at the right temperature, the sweet potato will cook for about 2 minutes per side, turning lightly golden brown.

Salt and Pepper Kettle Chips

Serves 4 / **Prep time:** 10 minutes / **Cook time:** 20 minutes

If I'm indulging in junk food, I want the best version imaginable. Making homemade potato chips is easier than you might think, and nothing compares to a fresh, hot, and crispy potato chip doused in salt and dunked in malt vinegar. I prefer russet potatoes because they get nice and crispy as they fry. If you don't own a mandoline slicer, experiment with thickness until you hit upon your perfect chip.

4 medium russet potatoes

4 cups canola oil

Fine sea salt

Finely ground
   black pepper

1. **Thinly slice the potatoes.** Peel the potatoes and cut them into very thin slices, either with a mandoline slicer or with a sharp chef's knife.

2. **Fry the chips.** In a Dutch oven over medium heat, heat the canola oil to 365°F (if you don't have a thermometer, lower 1 potato slice in the oil; when it bubbles and is golden, the oil is hot enough). While the oil comes to temperature, pat the potato slices with paper towels to wick away any moisture. Line a baking sheet with paper towels and place it near the Dutch oven. Working in small batches, fry the potato slices for about 3 minutes, until golden. Using a spider strainer or a slotted spoon, transfer the chips to the prepared pan to drain.

3. **Season the chips.** While the potatoes are still hot, sprinkle them generously with salt and pepper. Let cool completely, then store at room temperature in a sealed bag for up to 3 days. Season with additional salt before serving.

TECHNIQUE TIP: A long-handled, open-wire strainer called a *spider* is useful for deep-frying because you can remove food without transferring very much of the hot oil, and you can use it to shake away excess flour when dredging.

Coconut Shrimp

Serves 4 / **Prep time:** 10 minutes / **Cook time:** 20 minutes

This dish is definitely best fresh, but it can be frozen and reheated in the oven for crispy leftovers. The basic setup requires three bowls: Coat the shrimp in one bowl of seasoned flour, then coat them in a bowl of beaten egg, and then press them into a bowl of panko and coconut. You'll want the oil to come halfway up the food's sides as it lays flat, which will depend on the size of your Dutch oven; mine needed ½ cup of oil for this recipe.

⅓ cup all-purpose flour

½ teaspoon salt, plus
   more for seasoning

½ teaspoon freshly ground
   black pepper

2 large eggs

¾ cup panko bread crumbs

1 cup sweetened
   shredded coconut

1 pound large shrimp,
   peeled and deveined

½ cup refined coconut oil

1. **Set up the dipping bowls.** Set 3 shallow bowls on the counter. In the first, stir together the flour, salt, and pepper. In the second, whisk the eggs. In the third, combine the panko and shredded coconut.

2. **Coat the shrimp.** Dip the shrimp, one at a time, into the flour mixture, then the eggs, and finally the panko-coconut mixture, pressing to get a good amount of coconut on each shrimp. Place the coated shrimp on a plate.

3. **Heat the oil.** In a Dutch oven over medium heat, heat the oil to 365°F. If you don't have a thermometer, lower one shrimp into the hot oil. When it bubbles and turns golden brown, the oil is ready.

4. **Fry and serve.** Line a plate with paper towels, and set it aside. Working in batches of 6 shrimp at a time, fry the shrimp for about 3 minutes per side, until dark golden brown. Using a slotted spoon, transfer the cooked shrimp to the prepared plate and season with salt, if needed. Fried shrimp are best fresh, but you can refrigerate leftovers for up to 2 days.

Parmesan Parsley Fries

Serves 4 / Prep time: 10 minutes, plus 2 hours to soak / Cook time: 30 minutes

These herbaceous homemade French fries are without equal. The process makes you appreciate how much effort goes into so-called "fast food." Raw potatoes need to be cut into strips and soaked for 2 hours to remove some of their outside layer of starch. Then, after the potatoes are thoroughly dried, they get fried twice. It may sound odd, but it's necessary to fry, strain, and re-fry the potatoes to get the best texture on the inside as well as the outside.

4 russet potatoes

4 cups canola oil

Salt

Finely grated Parmesan cheese, for seasoning

1 bunch fresh parsley, minced

1. **Cut and soak the potatoes.** Peel the potatoes and cut them into thin planks. Stack the planks and cut them into thin strips. Place the cut pieces in a large bowl and pour in enough water to cover them completely. Refrigerate the soaked potato pieces for 2 hours.

2. **Drain and dry.** Drain the potatoes and lay them on a baking sheet. Blot them dry with a clean kitchen towel or paper towels.

3. **Heat the oil.** In a Dutch oven over medium heat, heat the canola oil to 365°F. If you don't have a thermometer, drop a single fry into the hot oil. When bubbles form all around the potato, the oil is ready.

4. **Fry, strain, refry, and serve.** Working in batches to avoid overcrowding the pot (and lowering the oil temperature), add the fries to the hot oil and fry for 5 minutes per batch. Spread the fried potatoes on a baking sheet. In batches again, return the potatoes to the oil to fry a second time for 3 to 5 minutes per batch, until golden. Drain the fries on a baking sheet lined with paper towels, and season with salt. Sprinkle generously with Parmesan and parsley. Dive in!

Pan-Fried Pork Bo Ssam

Serves 4 / **Prep time:** 10 minutes / **Cook time:** 15 minutes

Traditional Korean pork bo ssam (bossam) involves a lengthy process of cooking and shredding pork shoulder, as well as an extensive presentation of accompaniments and dipping sauces. As a time saver, ground pork captures the essence of the dish when it is panfried until caramelized. To season the pork, look for either gochujang or Sriracha and tame the spiciness with rice vinegar. Rather than a main course, I like to serve the lettuce-wrapped pork as an appetizer with a scoop of rice and kimchi.

2 tablespoons canola oil

1 pound ground pork

4 teaspoons light brown sugar

Pinch salt

2 scallions, thinly sliced

1 (2-inch) piece fresh ginger, peeled and finely grated

2 tablespoons hot sauce (such as Sriracha)

1 tablespoon rice vinegar

2 teaspoon tamari

2 heads butter lettuce

1. **Brown the pork.** In a Dutch oven over medium heat, heat the canola oil. Add the ground pork and sprinkle with the brown sugar and salt. Cook for 12 minutes, stirring occasionally with a spoon to break up the meat, until brown.

2. **Add accoutrements.** Turn off the heat and add the scallions, ginger, hot sauce, vinegar, and tamari. Stir well to coat the pork. Taste and adjust the seasoning as desired.

3. **Serve.** Place the lettuce leaves on a serving platter. Spoon some pork into each lettuce cup. Fold and enjoy. Refrigerate leftovers for up to 3 days.

INGREDIENT TIP: When grating fresh ginger, it's easier to work with a larger section than you need. Hold it firmly and rub it briskly against a zester. Collect the pulp with the juices.

Falafel with Easy Tahini

Serves 6 / **Prep time:** 15 minutes, plus overnight to soak / **Cook time:** 35 minutes

To make falafel, you must use uncooked, dried chickpeas that have been soaked overnight; canned or cooked chickpeas are too soft and will not work. To make a sticky mixture, combine the chickpeas with seasonings in the food processor, buzz it all up until the chickpeas are very finely chopped, and then shape the mixture into balls. Frying cooks the chickpeas and gives you a nice brown, crunchy exterior. You can serve the falafel over salad or in pita bread with a simple sauce made of lemon juice and tahini.

1 cup dried chickpeas, soaked in water overnight

1 shallot, roughly chopped

3 tablespoons fresh parsley, minced

3 garlic cloves, roughly chopped

2½ teaspoons salt

1 teaspoon ground cumin

1 teaspoon red pepper flakes

¾ teaspoon ground coriander

½ teaspoon baking powder

5 tablespoons chickpea (garbanzo) flour

Canola oil

1. **Desiccate the chickpeas.** Drain and rinse the soaked chickpeas, then transfer them to a food processor. Add the shallot, parsley, garlic, salt, cumin, red pepper flakes, and coriander. Pulse to form a sticky, coarse meal.

2. **Form the falafel balls.** Transfer the chickpea mixture to a medium bowl and mix in the baking powder and chickpea flour. Shape the falafel mixture into about 20 (1½-inch) balls.

3. **Heat the oil for frying.** Line a plate with paper towels and set aside. Pour enough canola oil into a Dutch oven to reach a 2-inch depth. Heat the oil slowly over medium heat to 365°F. If you don't have a thermometer, place a tester falafel ball into the oil. If the falafel turns brown after cooking for 4 minutes per side, the oil is ready.

4. **Fry the falafel.** Working in batches of 6 at a time, add the falafel to the hot oil and fry for 4 minutes per side, until browned. Using a slotted spoon, transfer the falafel to the prepared plate to drain. Serve warm. Refrigerate leftovers for up to 3 days.

TECHNICAL TIP: To soak the chickpeas, measure 1 cup of dried chickpeas into a medium bowl. Fill the bowl with water, and set it aside on the counter. After soaking overnight, the beans will have doubled in size; strain, rinse, and use them in the recipe within 24 hours.

Mozzarella Sticks

Serves 6 / **Prep time:** 10 minutes, plus 1 hour to freeze / **Cook time:** 35 minutes

These pan-fried golden cheese sticks are a huge hit and make the perfect side for pizza night. For that classic cheesy pull, freeze the mozzarella before frying. That way, the cheese doesn't melt before the coating crisps. To finish it off, you only need a side of warm marinara to offset the richness of the cheese.

2 large eggs

1 tablespoon milk

1 cup Italian-seasoned bread crumbs

¼ cup all-purpose flour

2 teaspoons garlic powder

1 pound mozzarella cheese, cut into ¾-by-¾-inch strips

1 cup canola oil

Salt

1. **Coat and freeze.** Line a baking sheet with parchment paper and set aside. In a small bowl, whisk the eggs and milk to combine. On a plate, stir together the bread crumbs, flour, and garlic powder. Dip the cheese sticks, one at a time, in the eggs, then roll in the flour and bread crumb mixture. Repeat, dipping in the eggs and bread crumbs again. Set the coated cheese sticks on the prepared baking sheet. Freeze for 1 hour.

2. **Heat the oil.** In a Dutch oven over medium heat, heat the oil to 365°F. If you don't have a thermometer, lower 1 mozzarella stick into the oil. When it is fully cooked in 2 minutes or less with a golden exterior and just melted interior, the oil is ready. Adjust the temperature of the oil accordingly.

3. **Fry and serve.** Working in batches, put a few mozzarella sticks in the oil and fry for about 1 minute per side or until golden. Remove quickly before the cheese starts to leak, transferring to the prepared baking sheet to drain. Season with salt. Refrigerate leftovers for up to 3 days. Rewarm in a 375°F oven for 10 minutes for the best texture.

Pan-Fried London Broil Steak

Serves 4 / **Prep time:** 10 minutes / **Cook time:** 20 minutes

This simply seasoned steak delivers a quick, easy, tender meal. I recommend a heavy-duty Dutch oven for pan-frying thick steak for two reasons: The tall sides prevent oil from splattering, and the metal does a good job of searing the beef evenly for a flavorful crust. This recipe proves that you don't need a long marinating time to produce a juicy steak—just some good old-fashioned butter, salt, and pepper.

2 pounds (1½ inches thick) boneless beef round London broil

1 tablespoon salt

1 tablespoon freshly ground black pepper

4 tablespoons (½ stick) unsalted butter

1. **Preheat the oven.** Preheat the oven to 350°F.

2. **Trim and season the steak.** Using a sharp knife, remove any connective tissue from the steak. Season the steak with salt and pepper.

3. **Cook the steak.** In a Dutch oven over medium heat, melt the butter. Set the steak in the hot butter. Cook for 3 minutes without moving. Flip the steak and finish it in the oven for 8 minutes. Let the steak sit in the Dutch oven for 5 minutes, then transfer to a cutting board. Cut the steak across the grain into thin slices and serve with a side salad, if desired. Refrigerate leftovers for up to 4 days.

TECHNICAL TIP: Use a meat thermometer to determine the doneness. For medium-rare, remove the steak from the heat at 130°F, as it will continue to rise in temperature as it rests.

Deep-Fried Chicken with Coriander and Cumin

Serves 6 / **Prep time:** 10 minutes / **Cook time:** 1 hour, plus 10 minutes to rest

Something about fried chicken reminds me of family cookouts. As a child more interested in playing than eating, you could hardly get me to sit down for a meal, but the smell of fried chicken was enough to stop me in my tracks. While I don't remember most childhood meals, I have countless memories of devouring piping-hot chicken thighs over paper plates with corn on the cob.

6 bone-in, skin-on
   chicken drumsticks
6 bone-in, skin-on
   chicken thighs
3 cups buttermilk
2 teaspoons plus
   1 tablespoon salt,
   divided, plus more
   for seasoning
1 teaspoon plus
   1 tablespoon freshly
   ground black
   pepper, divided
4 cups canola oil
3 cups all-purpose flour
½ cup cornstarch
1 tablespoon garlic powder
2 teaspoons
   ground coriander
1 teaspoon ground cumin

1. **Coat the chicken.** In a large bowl, combine the chicken pieces, buttermilk, 2 teaspoons of salt, and 1 teaspoon of pepper. Set aside while you heat the oil, or cover and refrigerate for up to 3 hours.

2. **Heat the oil.** In a Dutch oven over medium heat, heat the oil to 375°F.

3. **Bread and fry the chicken in batches.** In a large bowl, whisk together the flour, cornstarch, garlic powder, coriander, and cumin, as well as the remaining 1 tablespoon of salt and the remaining 1 tablespoon of pepper. Working one piece at a time, remove the chicken from the buttermilk, gently shake to remove the excess, and dip it into the flour mixture to coat thoroughly. Gently shake to remove the excess flour, then gently place the chicken in the hot oil. Working in batches of up to 3 pieces at a time, fry the chicken for about 14 minutes, turning with tongs, until the chicken is fully cooked (see tip).

4. **Drain and serve.** Line a baking sheet with paper towels. Transfer the cooked chicken to the prepared baking sheet. While it's still hot, season it with salt. Let rest for 10 minutes, then serve. Refrigerate leftovers for up to 3 days. Reheat in a 375°F oven for 15 minutes for the best texture.

TECHNICAL TIP: If you don't have a thermometer, dip one tip of a piece of chicken into the oil. If it doesn't bubble immediately, wait 2 minutes and try again. As soon as the batter turns golden, the oil is ready. Proceed with frying the batch.

Beer-Battered Tilapia

Serves 6 / **Prep time:** 15 minutes / **Cook time:** 25 minutes

This beer-battered fish recipe is customizable, easy, and delicious. Spices tend to get lost in flour, which is why it's necessary to salt the fried fish while it's still glistening hot. If you're concerned about the fish getting cold while you fry it in batches, hold the cooked fish in a warm oven. This fried fish is so tasty, it needs little more than tartar sauce on the side.

1½ cups all-purpose flour, divided

1 tablespoon salt, plus more for seasoning

2 teaspoons freshly ground black pepper

1 teaspoon baking powder

2 large eggs, cold

¾ cup cold beer

3 cups canola oil

1½ pounds skinless tilapia fillets, halved lengthwise into long strips

1. **Make the wet batter.** In a medium bowl, stir together 1 cup of flour, the salt, pepper, baking powder, eggs, and beer. Refrigerate while you heat the oil.

2. **Heat the oil.** In a Dutch oven over medium heat, heat the canola oil to 375°F.

3. **Dredge and dip the tilapia.** Put the remaining ½ cup of flour in a medium bowl. Place the cold wet batter next to it. Dredge the tilapia strips in flour, then dip them into the cold, wet batter, shaking to remove the excess.

4. **Fry and season.** Fry the tilapia, a few pieces at a time, in the hot oil for about 5 minutes, turning occasionally with tongs, until the coating is golden brown. Remove and immediately season with salt. Serve warm.

INGREDIENT TIP: I've experimented with different lagers, but I like the crisp, light flavor of Miller High Life for this beer batter.

TECHNICAL TIP: If you don't have a thermometer, once the tilapia has been battered, dip one tip of a fillet into the oil. If it doesn't bubble immediately, wait 2 minutes and try again. As soon as the batter turns golden, the oil is ready. Proceed with frying the batch.

Frybread Navajo Tacos

Serves 6 / **Prep time:** 10 minutes, plus 1 hour to rest / **Cook time:** 35 minutes

Navajo tacos are served open-face and enjoyed with a knife and fork. This is a no-knead frybread, made with only four ingredients. I generally use the bread as a base for beans, cheese, lettuce, and a warm red or green chile sauce, such as Mild Red Enchilada Sauce (page 122).

2 cups all-purpose flour, plus more for dusting

2½ teaspoons baking powder

½ teaspoon salt

¾ cup warm water

Canola oil

1 (16-ounce) can vegetarian refried pinto beans

½ cup shredded cheddar cheese

1 head iceberg lettuce, thinly sliced

Hot sauce, for serving (optional)

1. **Make the dough.** In a medium bowl, whisk the flour, baking powder, and salt to combine. Slowly stir in the warm water. Gather the dough in the center of the bowl to form a sticky ball. Cover with plastic wrap or a damp cloth and let rest for 1 hour.

2. **Roll.** Dust a work surface with flour. Divide the dough into 6 equal portions; roll each piece on the floured surface to a ¼-inch-thick circle.

3. **Heat the oil.** In a Dutch oven over medium heat, pour in enough canola oil to reach a 2-inch depth. Heat the oil to 350°F. If you don't have a thermometer, place a small piece of dough in the hot oil. When the dough floats and bubbles, the oil is ready.

4. **Fry the bread.** Line a plate with paper towels and set aside. Gently lower 1 or 2 pieces of flattened dough into the hot oil. Fry for about 3 minutes, until puffy and golden, turning the dough with tongs. Transfer to the prepared plate to drain.

5. **Make the tacos.** In a small microwave-safe bowl, microwave the pinto beans on high power for 1 minute. Stir and microwave for 1 minute more, until hot. Spread a layer of the hot beans on each frybread, then sprinkle with cheese and lettuce. Serve with hot sauce (if using) or a warm chile sauce, if desired.

BROILED GARLIC-HERB MASHED POTATOES, page 120

Sides and Sauces

CHAPTER SEVEN

What's the secret to preparing more satisfying meals at home? Well, to start, include sides and sauces for more flavor and contrast on the plate. Choose vibrant in-season vegetables—from spring peas to height-of-summer bell peppers to fall's budding Brussels sprouts. Whatever you choose, the Dutch oven's heat will extract their natural sweetness. This chapter explores the simple ways you can use olive oil, fresh herbs, toasted spices, and lemon juice to supply the finishing touches to vegetables and sauces alike.

Whether your main course is a starch, a protein, or a fat, it deserves dynamic, satisfying accompaniments. These sides and sauces are exactly what you want to create with your Dutch oven.

Roasted Bell Pepper Coulis

Makes 1½ cups / **Prep time:** 5 minutes / **Cook time:** 40 minutes

This bright orange sauce is a great way to add some zing and a fresh pop of color to soup, fish, or chicken. A coulis is one of the easiest sauces to make because it's just a thin puree of fruit or vegetables; this one has a smoky, roasted pepper flavor that's slightly spicy and sweet. If you're feeling artistic, transfer the sauce to a squeeze bottle to create swirls or zigzags on finished dishes. For peak flavor, buy bell peppers between July and September.

2 red bell peppers

¾ cup water

3 tablespoons olive oil, plus more as needed

2 teaspoons hot sauce, plus more as needed

½ teaspoon salt, plus more as needed

1. **Preheat the oven.** Preheat the oven to 475°F.

2. **Roast the peppers.** Place the whole bell peppers in the Dutch oven and roast on the middle rack, uncovered, for about 40 minutes or until very tender.

3. **Steam.** Remove the peppers from the oven, set the Dutch oven on the stovetop, and cover the pot with the lid. Let the bell peppers steam for 5 minutes. This makes it easier to peel away the waxy skin. The peppers will be very hot, so let them cool before handling. Once cool, discard the stem and seeds. Peel away the skin to reveal the sweet pepper flesh underneath.

4. **Blend.** In a blender or food processor, combine the roasted peppers, water, olive oil, hot sauce, and salt. Puree until completely smooth and lump free. Taste and adjust the salt, fat, acid, or heat based on how you want to serve the sauce. Use warm or cool. Refrigerate leftovers for up to 1 week.

Vegetable Crudités Platter

Serves 6 / Prep time: 15 minutes / Cook time: 10 minutes

An enticing crudités platter is all about presenting the vegetables as the crisp and welcome appetizer they are. I like to briefly boil the vegetables and plunge them into ice water. Blanching and shocking the vegetables increases their vibrancy while maintaining that snappy bite that makes raw vegetables so clean tasting and refreshing.

1 (2-pound) bag multicolor carrots

1 bunch red radishes

1 bunch broccolini

1 head cauliflower

3 tablespoons salt

1 teaspoon white wine vinegar

1. **Trim the vegetables.** Peel and quarter the carrots lengthwise to preserve their natural shape. Put the radishes in a medium bowl and cover them with water. Scrub the radishes to remove dirt, lifting the radishes in and out of the water to leave the sand behind. Halve the radishes (if your radishes have their greens attached, leave 1 inch of the stem attached). Trim the broccolini into florets about 4 inches long. Cut the cauliflower into large florets with 2-inch stems.

2. **Blanch and shock.** Fill a Dutch oven halfway with water and bring it to a boil over high heat. Add the salt and vinegar to the water to bring out the best color and flavor from the vegetables. Place a large bowl on the counter near the stovetop and fill it with ice and water. Working by type, add the vegetables to the boiling water and cook for just 20 seconds. Using a slotted spoon, immediately transfer the vegetables to the ice bath to prevent further cooking.

3. **Serve.** To serve the vegetables (and keep them nice and crisp), let the Dutch oven cool, then fill the bottom with ice. Arrange the vegetables attractively on top of the ice and serve with Artichoke Dip (page 127), Hatch Chile Nacho Cheese Sauce (page 126), or other favorite dips. Alternatively, refrigerate the vegetables in the Dutch oven, up to 1 day in advance, until you are ready to serve.

TECHNICAL TIP: When serving crudités, keep in mind that people need to be able to hold on to the vegetables while dipping them, so it's important to leave the vegetables longer in length than you normally would—3 or 4 inches.

Sautéed Garlic Bok Choy

Serves 4 / **Prep time:** 10 minutes / **Cook time:** 10 minutes

This lemon-finished bok choy makes a fast, easy, and delicious vegetable side for fish or topping for rice. As soon as you add the bok choy, just step away for a minute because you don't want to disturb them. Within a couple of minutes, the bok choy will begin to caramelize around the edges, which makes the dish extra delicious.

6 heads baby bok choy

2 tablespoons olive oil

½ teaspoon salt

4 garlic cloves, minced

Pinch red pepper flakes

Juice of ½ lemon (optional)

1. **Trim the bok choy.** Remove the stem ends of the bok choy heads, leaving the whites still attached. If your bok choy are small, quarter each head. If they are large, roughly chop the heads into large pieces.

2. **Sauté the bok choy.** In a Dutch oven over medium heat, heat the olive oil until it spreads and glistens. Spread the bok choy over the oil and sprinkle with salt. Cook without stirring for at least 2 minutes, until the bottoms begin to brown. Add the garlic and red pepper flakes and toss to coat. Cook, undisturbed, for 2 minutes more, just until the garlic begins to turn slightly golden and the green leaves are completely wilted.

3. **Serve with lemon.** Taste and squeeze the lemon juice on top (if using). Serve warm. Refrigerate leftovers for up to 3 days.

TECHNICAL TIP: People often think you must stir vegetables right away when sautéing. However, if your goal is caramelization, it's generally better to let them sit for a moment in the hot oil and stir only every so often.

Roasted Brussels Sprouts with Harissa

Serves 4 / **Prep time:** 10 minutes / **Cook time:** 25 minutes

Harissa is an aromatic chile paste condiment that is especially popular in North African and Middle Eastern cuisines. Although its intensity varies greatly from brand to brand, some harissa really packs a punch, so taste it before you add too much to the roasted Brussels sprouts. I've had harissa so spicy that it required only a dab, and I've had some mild enough to eat by itself. Mina brand makes both mild and spicy harissa that are delicious.

1½ pounds Brussels
   sprouts, trimmed
   and halved
2 tablespoons olive oil
½ teaspoon salt
Harissa, for seasoning
1 lemon

1. **Preheat the oven.** Preheat the oven to 425°F.

2. **Prepare the Brussels sprouts.** In a Dutch oven, toss together the Brussels sprouts, olive oil, and salt. Spread the sprouts in an even layer.

3. **Roast until tender and brown.** Roast the Brussels sprouts, uncovered, for about 22 minutes, until the edges start to crisp and brown. Remove the pot from the oven and toss the Brussels sprouts with harissa to taste. Grate the zest of the lemon over the top. Then, cut the lemon in half and add a spritz of lemon juice. Serve warm. Refrigerate leftovers for up to 4 days.

MAKE IT CLASSIC: Instead of the harissa, finely grate Parmesan cheese over the roasted Brussels sprouts just before serving.

Broiled Garlic-Herb Mashed Potatoes

Serves 6 / **Prep time:** 10 minutes / **Cook time:** 35 minutes

A ricer is a fantastic tool for creating really fluffy mashed potatoes, but you can still get a nice texture by mashing. Before adding the butter, I warm it and let it sit with garlic and fresh herbs to extract those flavors. That way, the mashed potatoes take on the essence of the herbs and garlic.

3 pounds russet potatoes, peeled and cubed

1 tablespoon salt, plus more for seasoning

6 tablespoons unsalted butter, divided

5 garlic cloves, minced

2 thyme sprigs

2 rosemary sprigs

Freshly ground black pepper

1. **Boil the potatoes.** Put the potatoes in a large pot with the salt. Cover with water and bring to a boil over high heat. Cook for about 20 minutes, until the potatoes are fork-tender. Place a colander in the sink and drain the potatoes.

2. **Infuse the butter.** Meanwhile, in the Dutch oven over low heat, melt 5 tablespoons of butter. Add the garlic, thyme, and rosemary. Cook, stirring occasionally, for 1 minute. Turn off the heat and set the pot aside.

3. **Press the potatoes.** Using a ricer, press the warm potatoes through the fine holes into the large pot that you cooked them in. Season with salt and pepper.

4. **Broil.** Melt the remaining 1 tablespoon of butter in a small bowl in the microwave. Position an oven rack as close as you can get to the broiler while still allowing enough headroom for your Dutch oven to fit. Preheat the broiler. Remove and discard the thyme and rosemary sprigs from the infused butter in the Dutch oven. Pour the riced potatoes into the Dutch oven. Using a spatula, gently fold the potatoes into the butter to combine. Brush the top with the remaining melted butter, then place the Dutch oven directly under the broiler. Broil until the top is golden brown, which could take anywhere from 4 to 15 minutes, depending on how close the food sits to your broiler—keep a close eye on it.

TECHNICAL TIP: If your mashed potatoes tend to be gluey, you could be overmixing or overmashing them.

Mild Red Enchilada Sauce

Makes 3½ cups / **Prep time:** 10 minutes / **Cook time:** 10 minutes

I strive for balance in my enchilada sauce and go to a lot of trouble to use quality ingredients. Because this sauce depends on the chili powder's freshness, I recommend replacing this spice in your cupboard every 4 months. Chili powder made from New Mexico chiles is my favorite for red enchilada sauce because its flavor is uniquely mild and fruity.

2 tablespoons lard, such as bacon grease

¼ cup mild chili powder

1 tablespoon ground cumin

1 teaspoon garlic powder

½ teaspoon dried oregano

1 (15-ounce) can tomato sauce

1½ cups beef stock

2 teaspoons cornstarch

1 teaspoon salt

1. **Gently warm the spices.** In a Dutch oven over medium heat, melt the lard. Add the chili powder, cumin, garlic powder, and oregano. Cook, stirring, for about 1 minute to let the lard get hot, then add the tomato sauce.

2. **Thicken the sauce.** In a liquid measuring cup, whisk the beef stock and cornstarch well to create a slurry. Immediately add the slurry to the tomato mixture. Increase the heat to medium-high and cook for about 5 minutes, stirring well, until the sauce bubbles and thickens slightly. Add the salt and use right away, or cool and refrigerate for up to 4 days.

INGREDIENT TIP: Over the years, I've found that the best lard is the kind you make at home. Strain bacon grease into a mason jar, or reserve pork drippings from a roast. Of course, the enchilada sauce will still be perfectly good if you want to substitute mild olive oil or vegetable oil instead.

Smoky Paprika Cream Sauce

Makes ¾ cup / **Prep time:** 5 minutes / **Cook time:** 5 minutes

Fresh lemon and smoked paprika give this velvety smooth cream sauce just the right amount of oomph to make a bowl of fusilli or chicken exciting. Compared to regular paprika, smoked paprika has a more savory profile. You'll notice that this cream sauce requires no flour for thickening; that's because even a small amount of lemon juice has the power to thicken heavy cream.

3 tablespoons unsalted butter

½ teaspoon grated lemon zest

2½ teaspoons smoked paprika

½ teaspoon salt

¼ cup chicken stock

2 tablespoons freshly squeezed lemon juice

⅓ cup heavy cream, plus more as needed

1. **Start the sauce.** In a Dutch oven over medium heat, melt the butter until bubbly, then add the lemon zest, paprika, and salt. Cook, stirring, for 1 minute, then add the chicken stock and bring to a simmer.

2. **Incorporate the cream.** Turn off the heat and add the lemon juice and heavy cream. At this point, if you want to thicken the sauce, simmer while whisking for a few minutes; for a thinner sauce, add more cream. Serve warm. Refrigerate leftovers for up to 5 days.

Easy Caramel Sauce

Makes 1 cup / Prep time: 5 minutes / Cook time: 10 minutes

Make a batch of this caramel sauce when you want something sweet, salty, and irresistibly buttery. You won't need a candy thermometer here, just a heat-resistant wooden spoon or rubber spatula to help you stir. For a quick snack, let the caramel thicken a bit in the refrigerator, then serve it as a dip with green apple slices.

1 cup sugar

3 tablespoons water

½ cup heavy cream

4 tablespoons (½ stick) unsalted butter

½ teaspoon salt

1. **Caramelize the sugar.** In a Dutch oven over medium heat, combine the sugar and water. Bring the mixture to a simmer without stirring (stirring can cause the melted sugar to recrystallize). The sugar will dissolve very slowly at first and eventually bubble and melt into a clear liquid. Once the sugar dissolves, cook for about 3 minutes; the sugar will develop a delicious caramel aroma and amber color. Immediately turn off the heat and stir in the heavy cream. Stir continuously for about 1 minute. It's okay if the sugar seizes (turns solid) a bit at this point.

2. **Stir in the butter.** Add the butter. While stirring constantly, let the butter melt into the sugar until you have a smooth, unified sauce. Stir in the salt, and let the sauce cool completely before tasting. Refrigerate the caramel in a sealed mason jar for up to 1 month. It will thicken as it cools, so you may need to warm it before each use.

TECHNICAL TIP: You can easily fix crystallized sugar. Add ¼ cup water, and bring the sugar back to a boil. Water will help the crystals dissolve, allowing you to proceed with the melting process.

Chipotle Black Beans

Serves 6 / **Prep time:** 10 minutes / **Cook time:** 10 minutes

Beans are the ultimate quick and easy side dish, especially when simmered with something bold and smoky like a dried chipotle chile. I prefer to use canned beans here, which are already cooked and absorb plenty of flavor rapidly. Serve these alongside Cheese Enchiladas in Red Sauce (page 76).

2 dried chipotle
chiles or 1 teaspoon
chipotle powder

2 tablespoons olive oil

1 white onion,
finely chopped

2 garlic cloves, minced

2 teaspoons ground cumin

1½ teaspoons salt, plus
more for seasoning

2 (15-ounce) cans
black beans, drained
and rinsed

Freshly squeezed
lime juice, for
seasoning (optional)

1. **Toast the chiles.** In a Dutch oven over medium heat, cook the chiles for 30 seconds or until fragrant, pressing them down into the pan and turning them with tongs.

2. **Sweat the onion and simmer the beans.** Add the olive oil and onion and cook for about 5 minutes, until very soft, stirring frequently. Once the onion is soft, stir in the garlic, cumin, and salt. Add the black beans. Simmer for at least 5 minutes to really get the chipotle essence into the beans. Taste and season with lime juice (if using) and more salt as desired. Remove and discard the chiles. Refrigerate leftovers for up to 2 days.

VARIATION TIP: If you can't find dried chipotle chiles, add 1 or 2 canned chipotles in adobo sauce. There's no need to toast them, so add them with the onion in step 2.

Hatch Chile Nacho Cheese Sauce

Makes 1¾ cups / **Prep time:** 10 minutes / **Cook time:** 10 minutes

When it comes to nachos, I'm insatiable. What often begins as a "snack" usually turns into a meal of tortilla chips and this ultra-cheesy chile sauce. It's thick and creamy and speckled with mild bits of roasted pepper. Grab some chips, turn on Netflix, and dive in!

2 tablespoons
   unsalted butter
2 tablespoons
   all-purpose flour
1½ cups whole milk
1 cup shredded
   cheddar cheese
¾ teaspoon salt
1 (4-ounce) can diced
   Hatch chiles

1. **Make a roux.** In a Dutch oven over medium heat, melt the butter. Add the flour and cook, stirring constantly, for 1 minute, until the mixture turns tan in color. Add the milk and cook, stirring, for about 1 minute, just until the mixture thickens.

2. **Melt the cheese.** Turn off the heat and add the cheese and salt. Stir until the cheese is melted and the sauce is smooth. Stir in the chiles. For the best texture, serve the sauce immediately over tortilla chips or as a dip for bread or the Vegetable Crudités Platter (page 116).

VARIATION TIP: A cheese dip is a great way to experiment with different cheese and pepper combinations. For a pimiento cheese sauce, try jarred or canned pimiento peppers with cheddar and a touch of cream cheese.

Artichoke Dip

Serves 8 / **Prep time:** 10 minutes / **Cook time:** 15 minutes

This baked artichoke dip is easy to whip up and a total crowd-pleaser. Serve it warm or cool with anything crunchy, such as a Vegetable Crudités Platter (page 116), little toasts, or pita chips. It's the perfect side for a party and can be served right out of the Dutch oven, or you can transfer it to serving bowls for easy nibbling.

2 (14-ounce) cans artichoke hearts, drained and rinsed

2 cups mayonnaise

2 cups finely grated Parmesan cheese

1 teaspoon freshly squeezed lemon juice

½ teaspoon garlic powder

1. **Preheat the oven.** Preheat the oven to 350°F.

2. **Mix and bake.** Roughly chop the artichoke hearts, place them in a Dutch oven, and stir in the mayonnaise, Parmesan, lemon juice, and garlic powder to combine. Smooth the top. Bake for about 15 minutes, until golden brown around the edges and bubbly. Serve warm or cool. Refrigerate leftovers for up to 4 days.

VARIATION TIP: While I prefer full-fat mayonnaise, you could replace the mayonnaise with a mixture of 1 cup of cream cheese and 1 cup of either sour cream or plain Greek yogurt for a similar texture.

Breads

CHAPTER EIGHT

Making bread from scratch is one of the most rewarding and engaging baking endeavors: It requires using your hands and feeling the texture of your ingredients. I like listening to music as I knead and often find myself completely immersed in the rhythm of kneading, shaping, and baking dough. Bread bakes differently in the Dutch oven—yeast breads get crunchy, golden crusts because the heat from the pot is right up against the sides of the bread, causing the texture to become drier and crunchier; enriched breads taste even sweeter because the hot walls of the Dutch oven increase the caramelization of the dough's sugar content. Whether you want the convenience of a quick bread or the joy of a slowly developed yeast bread, this chapter will help you experience bread baking on a whole new level.

Jalapeño Corn Bread with Honey Butter

Serves 10 / **Prep time:** 10 minutes / **Cook time:** 20 minutes

When I start a pot of Vegetarian Three-Bean Chili (page 65), I always get a hankering for this soft, slightly sweet, buttery cornbread. I like to let the chili simmer while the cornbread bakes so everything is ready at about the same time. I like how the jalapeño slices bake into the batter and the edges of the cornbread get crispy in the oven.

1 cup cornmeal

1 cup all-purpose flour

1 teaspoon baking powder

½ teaspoon baking soda

½ teaspoon salt

1 jalapeño pepper

1 scallion, thinly sliced

1 large egg

1 cup buttermilk

¼ cup packed light
brown sugar

8 tablespoons (1 stick)
unsalted butter, melted,
plus more for preparing
the Dutch oven

Honey, for serving

1. **Preheat the oven.** Preheat the oven to 425°F.

2. **Mix the dry ingredients.** In a medium bowl, whisk the cornmeal, flour, baking powder, baking soda, and salt. Set aside.

3. **Add the jalapeño and scallion.** Halve and seed the jalapeño. Thinly slice one half and set aside for the topping; mince the remaining half. Add the minced jalapeño and the scallion to the dry ingredients.

4. **Mix the wet ingredients.** In another medium bowl, whisk the egg, buttermilk, brown sugar, and melted butter. Pour the wet mixture into the dry ingredients and lightly stir with a spatula just until blended.

5. **Bake.** Coat a Dutch oven with melted butter. Pour the batter into the prepared Dutch oven, tilting the pot from side to side until the batter lays flat along the bottom. Arrange the reserved jalapeño slices on top. Bake for about 20 minutes, until golden brown and a tester inserted into the center of the bread comes out clean. Using a spatula, cut the bread into slices and serve warm with honey. Refrigerate leftovers, wrapped in plastic wrap, for up to 3 days.

Soft-Baked Pretzel Rolls

Serves 8 / **Prep time:** 20 minutes, plus 1 hour 20 minutes to rise and rest /
Cook time: 25 minutes

Making pretzels has never been easier! The dough is formed into rolls, boiled, and then baked for that pretzel sheen everybody loves. Scoring the dough with a knife creates a vent for the dough to expand as it cooks. I like to serve these warm with mustard or Hatch Chile Nacho Cheese Sauce (page 126) or cut them in half to make ham sandwiches.

2½ teaspoons active
   dry yeast

1¼ cups lukewarm water

1 tablespoon pure
   maple syrup

3¾ cups all-purpose flour

3 tablespoons unsalted
   butter, melted

1½ teaspoons salt

5 cups water

3 tablespoons baking soda

Coarse sea salt

1. **Form and knead the pretzel dough.** In a large bowl, stir together the yeast, warm water, and maple syrup. Let sit for 5 minutes, until the mixture begins to bubble, which tells you the yeast is active. Add the flour, melted butter, and salt. Stir to combine, then knead the dough in the bowl for 3 minutes to form a smooth ball. Cover the bowl with a clean cloth and let the dough rise in a warm place for about 1 hour, until doubled in size.

2. **Shape the rolls.** Portion the dough into 8 balls and set them on a sheet of parchment paper. Form a circle with your thumb and fingertips like you're making the okay sign. Push each roll through the circle and return it to the parchment. This creates tension across the surface of the dough to form a tall rounded shape. Cover the rolls and let rest for 20 minutes.

3. **Preheat the oven.** Preheat the oven to 425°F.

4. **Boil the rolls.** In a Dutch oven over high heat, combine the water and baking soda and bring to a boil. Gently slip 2 rolls into the boiling water and cook for 20 seconds on each side. Prevent the rolls from sticking to the bottom of the pot with a slotted spoon. Transfer the boiled rolls back to the parchment paper. Repeat with the remaining rolls. Empty the Dutch oven and let air-dry.

5. **Bake.** Sprinkle the rolls with coarse sea salt and cut a shallow X into the top of each roll using a sharp knife. Transfer the parchment paper with the rolls into the Dutch oven. It's okay if the rolls touch. Bake for about 20 minutes, until the tops are golden brown. Store at room temperature, wrapped in plastic wrap or aluminum foil, for up to 2 days, or freeze in sealed bags for up to 1 month.

Pull-Apart Herbed Dinner Rolls

Serves 12 / **Prep time:** 30 minutes, plus 2 hours 10 minutes to rise and rest /
Cook time: 15 minutes

The name of the game for these delectable rolls is waiting. You'll notice that, after the first rise, there's an additional rise—don't skip this step. With yeast rolls, you really can't rush the yeast while it's working away at building those air pockets that create those delectably light dinner rolls.

1 cup lukewarm water

1½ teaspoons active
dry yeast

2 teaspoons sugar

½ cup bread flour

1 cup pastry flour, divided

2 tablespoons olive oil,
plus more for preparing
the Dutch oven
and brushing

2 teaspoons salt

2 teaspoons chopped
fresh herbs, such as
rosemary, thyme,
or parsley

1 cup all-purpose flour,
plus more for dusting
and kneading

1. **Make the sponge.** In a large bowl, stir together the warm water, yeast, sugar, bread flour, and ½ cup of pastry flour until a thick batter forms. Cover the bowl with plastic wrap and set it aside in a warm place for 30 minutes or until the mixture is bubbly, an indication that the yeast is active.

2. **Form the dough.** Stir in the olive oil, salt, and herbs. Add the remaining ½ cup of pastry flour and stir to combine. Add the all-purpose flour and stir well until the dough pulls away from the sides of the bowl.

3. **Knead.** Lightly coat a Dutch oven with olive oil. Set aside. Dust a work surface with all-purpose flour and transfer the dough to the prepared surface. Knead the dough for 15 minutes, gradually adding just enough flour until the dough is smooth and no longer sticky. Transfer the smooth dough to the prepared Dutch oven, cover the pot with the lid, and let the dough rise in a warm place for about 45 minutes, until doubled in size.

4. **Rise again.** Fold and reshape the dough into a ball, cover, and let rise again for 45 minutes more.

5. **Shape and bake the rolls.** Preheat the oven to 350°F. Form the dough into 12 roughly equal round balls. Line the Dutch oven with parchment paper and arrange the rolls on top. Cover the pot and let rest for 10 minutes. Lightly brush the tops of the rolls with olive oil. Bake for about 15 minutes, until golden and firm to the touch. Lift the edges of the parchment to remove the rolls from the Dutch oven and serve slightly warm. Store at room temperature, in a sealed plastic bag, for up to 2 days, or freeze in sealed bags for up to 1 month.

TECHNICAL TIP: In winter, create a warm environment for bread dough to rise by turning the oven to 350°F for 1 minute. Be sure to turn off the oven before placing the dough inside.

Braided Saffron Challah

Serves 8 / **Prep time:** 30 minutes, plus 2 hours 20 minutes to rise and rest / **Cook time:** 50 minutes

Challah is characterized as an enriched bread because it contains fat from eggs and butter. It's easy to make but requires extra time to rise between steps because the fat slows down the yeast. I like how the unusual flavor of saffron straddles sweet and savory in this loaf, reflecting challah's unique status in both sweet and savory applications.

1 cup lukewarm water

¼ cup sugar

1½ teaspoons active
   dry yeast

Pinch saffron threads

3 large eggs, divided

1 large egg yolk

4 tablespoons (½ stick)
   unsalted butter, melted

1½ teaspoons salt

3½ cups all-purpose flour,
   plus more for dusting
   and kneading

1 tablespoon olive oil

1 tablespoon water

1. **Mix, knead, and rise.** In a medium bowl, stir together the warm water, sugar, yeast, and saffron. Let the mixture sit for 15 minutes, until it looks frothy, an indication the yeast is active. Incorporate 2 eggs, the egg yolk, melted butter, and salt into the yeast mixture, mixing well. Gradually add the flour, mixing as you go to form a soft, sticky dough. Dust a work surface with flour and transfer the dough to the prepared surface. Knead the dough for about 10 minutes, gradually adding up to 1 additional cup of flour if needed, until you have a smooth, elastic dough. Coat a medium bowl with olive oil, then set the dough inside and turn it to coat in the oil. Cover the bowl with a clean kitchen towel and let the dough rise in a warm place for 1 hour, until doubled in size.

2. **Second rise.** Turn and fold the dough. Re-cover the bowl and let rise for 1 hour more, again allowing the dough to double in size.

3. **Preheat the oven and braid the bread.** Preheat the oven to 350°F. Divide the dough into 3 equal pieces to make a braid. Roll each piece into a 2-by-20-inch rope. Pinch the ropes at the top and braid the dough, weaving the strands together to form the loaf. Line a Dutch oven with parchment paper and set the braided loaf inside, curving the loaf to fit the shape of your Dutch oven. Cover the pot with the lid and let the dough rest for 20 minutes, until doubled in size.

4. **Bake the bread.** Remove the lid and place the pot on the middle rack. Bake for 40 minutes, until the internal temperature of the bread is between 190°F and 205°F—the outside of the bread will be light brown and have a hollow sound when tapped. In a small bowl, whisk the remaining egg and water to create an egg wash. Brush the bread with the egg wash and bake for 5 to 10 minutes more. Let the bread cool completely before slicing. Store the loaf at room temperature, wrapped in plastic wrap or aluminum foil, for up to 2 days, or slice and freeze in sealable plastic bags for up to 1 month.

Whole-Wheat Bread

Serves 8 / **Prep time:** 40 minutes, plus 1 hour 15 minutes to rise / **Cook time:** 1 hour

What makes this such a wholesome loaf is the sweet, nutty flavor from the bran found in whole-wheat flours. The trick with whole-wheat bread is to balance the protein and fiber; this is why I mix whole-wheat bread flour (higher in protein) with whole-wheat pastry flour (lighter in texture). I like to begin this dough by making a "sponge," which gives extra time for the bran to hydrate and helps build flavor. With enough kneading, you will get a springy, chewy loaf that slices well for sandwiches.

1 tablespoon active
   dry yeast

2 cups lukewarm water

1 cup whole-wheat
   bread flour

4½ cups whole-wheat
   pastry flour, divided,
   plus more for dusting
   and kneading

3 tablespoons pure
   maple syrup

½ cup olive oil, plus more
   for preparing the bowl

1 tablespoon salt

1. **Make the sponge.** In a large bowl, stir together the yeast, warm water, bread flour, 1 cup of pastry flour, and the maple syrup to form a thick, wet batter. Cover the bowl with plastic wrap and set it aside in a warm place for 30 minutes or until the mixture is bubbly, an indication that the yeast is active.

2. **Make the dough and knead.** Add 3 cups of pastry flour, the olive oil, and the salt to the sponge. Stir to combine. Dust the counter with some of the remaining ½ cup of pastry flour, and turn the dough out onto the prepared surface. Knead the dough for about 10 minutes, until smooth, adding the remaining pastry flour only if needed (if it's sticking to the work surface or your hands) and just enough so that the dough is no longer sticky. The dough will be very sticky at first but will become stretchy and smooth as you work it. Coat a large bowl with olive oil and transfer the dough to it. Cover the bowl with plastic wrap and let the dough rise in a warm place for 1 hour or until doubled in size.

3. **Preheat the oven.** Preheat the oven to 375°F. Line a Dutch oven with parchment paper.

4. **Fold and rise again.** Fold the dough and smooth it into a ball. Transfer to the Dutch oven, cover the pot with the lid, and let rise for 15 minutes more.

5. **Score and bake the bread.** Using a sharp knife, make 3 shallow cuts across the top of the loaf. Bake, uncovered, for 1 hour or until the internal temperature of the dough is between 190°F and 205°F—the loaf will be brown and firm to the touch. Let the bread cool for at least 30 minutes before slicing. Store at room temperature, wrapped in plastic wrap or aluminum foil, for up to 2 days, or slice and freeze for up to 1 month.

VARIATION TIP: Add 1/3 cup of nuts or seeds in step 2. While I generally encourage experimentation, swapping flours can drastically change the chewiness, springiness, and hydration of this loaf.

Olive Bread

Serves 8 / **Prep time:** 20 minutes, plus 1 hour 30 minutes to rise / **Cook time:** 30 minutes

I go through periods when I crave olive bread. There's just something about the salty, briny Kalamata olives combined with this part-white, part-whole-wheat bread that hits the spot. Usually I serve it toasted with a smear of butter for breakfast or a salty snack.

1 cup lukewarm water

2½ teaspoons active
   dry yeast

½ teaspoon sugar

3 tablespoons olive oil,
   plus more for preparing
   the Dutch oven

¼ cup chopped pitted
   Kalamata olives

1 tablespoon salt

1 cup bread flour

2½ cups whole-wheat
   pastry flour, divided

1. **Proof the yeast.** In a medium bowl, stir together the warm water, yeast, and sugar. Let the mixture sit for about 5 minutes, until foamy, an indication that the yeast is active.

2. **Form the dough.** Stir in the olive oil, olives, salt, and bread flour. Add 2 cups of whole-wheat pastry flour and stir well until the dough pulls away from the sides of the bowl.

3. **Knead.** Lightly coat a Dutch oven with olive oil. Set aside. Dust a work surface with the remaining ½ cup of whole-wheat pastry flour and turn the dough out onto the prepared surface. Knead the dough for 15 minutes, gradually adding the remaining pastry flour until the dough is smooth. Transfer the dough to the prepared Dutch oven, cover the pot with the lid, and let the dough rise in a warm place for about 45 minutes, until doubled in size.

4. **Rise again.** Fold and reshape the dough into a ball, return it to the Dutch oven, cover the pot, and let the dough rise for 45 minutes more.

5. **Preheat the oven and bake.** Preheat the oven to 475°F. Lift the dough out of the Dutch oven, line the pot with a piece of parchment paper, and then return the dough to the pot. Cover and bake for about 30 minutes, until golden and firm to the touch. Let the bread cool completely before slicing. Store at room temperature, wrapped in plastic wrap or aluminum foil, for up to 2 days, or slice and freeze the bread for up to 1 month.

TECHNICAL TIP: It's important to cool the bread before slicing; there is residual gas in the bread that makes it less digestible, and cutting the bread too early compresses the crumb.

Rosemary Focaccia with Grapes

Serves 8 / Prep time: 35 minutes, plus 1 hour to rise / Cook time: 25 minutes

This Italian bread is shaped inside the Dutch oven and then drizzled liberally with olive oil and sprinkled with salt. I like to dimple the surface with my fingertips and then stuff the indented dough with rosemary and grapes before baking. This attractive flatbread can be eaten as a snack or served as an accompaniment to salads. At first glance, the ingredient list seems long, but you're mostly using pantry staples and likely have everything you need to get started.

FOR THE SPONGE

1 tablespoon active
   dry yeast
1 tablespoon honey
⅔ cup lukewarm water
½ cup bread flour

FOR THE FOCACCIA

1 small russet potato
½ cup lukewarm water
¼ cup plus 1 tablespoon
   olive oil, divided, plus
   more for preparing the
   Dutch oven
1 tablespoon sea salt, plus
   more for seasoning
1 cup bread flour
2 cups all-purpose flour,
   plus more for dusting
1 cup seedless
   purple grapes
Leaves from 2 fresh
   rosemary branches

1. **Make the sponge.** In a medium bowl, stir together the yeast, honey, warm water, and bread flour to form a wet batter. Cover the bowl with a clean kitchen towel and set it aside in a warm place for 20 minutes or until bubbly, an indication that the yeast is active.

2. **Make the focaccia.** Pierce the potato with a sharp knife, then microwave it on high power for 5 minutes. Turn the potato and microwave for 5 minutes more, until tender. Set the potato aside until it is completely cool, then peel and mash it. Add the mashed potato, warm water, ¼ cup of olive oil, and the salt to the sponge. Stir to combine. While stirring, sprinkle in the bread flour and all-purpose flour, stirring to form a very sticky, wet dough.

3. **Knead the dough.** Lightly dust a work surface with all-purpose flour and turn the dough out onto the prepared surface. Knead the dough by stretching and folding—it will be very sticky and wet at first, but it will become increasingly manageable as the gluten develops. Work the dough with your hands for about 10 minutes, until it has a wet but stretchy consistency.

4. **Let the dough rise.** Lightly coat a Dutch oven with olive oil. Transfer the dough to the prepared Dutch oven, cover the pot with the lid, and let the dough rise in a warm place for about 1 hour, until doubled in size.

5. **Season and bake the bread.** Preheat the oven to 475°F. Spread the dough in the bottom of the Dutch oven. Using your fingertips, dimple the surface, pressing down deep into the dough. Press the grapes and rosemary leaves into the dough. Drizzle the dough with the remaining 1 tablespoon of olive oil and season with salt. Bake, uncovered, for 25 minutes. There will be juices on the top of the bread where the grapes have burst and the sugars have caramelized, and the top will have a slightly golden color. It will be soft and chewy. Remove the focaccia from the Dutch oven; let it cool for 5 minutes before slicing and serving. Because of the grapes, this bread is best served fresh. However, it will keep in the refrigerator for up to 3 days. For the best texture, rewarm refrigerated focaccia in the oven before eating.

MAKE IT CLASSIC: Omit the grapes and rosemary and make a plain focaccia with salt and pepper, or top it with thin slivers of red onion before baking.

TECHNICAL TIP: Reserve half of the dough in the refrigerator and bake it the next day if your Dutch oven is too small to accommodate all of the dough at once.

American-Irish Soda Bread with Raisins

Serves 8 / **Prep time:** 20 minutes / **Cook time:** 45 minutes

Making quick bread provides such a sense of satisfaction and accomplishment, despite requiring so little effort. I cherish the Dutch oven's unique ability to turn dough leavened merely with baking soda and buttermilk into this incredibly golden, crusty loaf. I include eggs and butter for richness and a dense, soft crumb speckled with chewy raisins. For a scrumptious snack or dessert, serve this bread warm with butter.

4⅓ cups all-purpose flour

1 teaspoon baking soda

1½ teaspoons salt

5 tablespoons cold
   unsalted butter

1 cup raisins

1¾ cups buttermilk

1 large egg

4 tablespoons raw
   granulated cane
   sugar, divided

1. **Preheat the oven.** Preheat the oven to 400°F. Line a Dutch oven with parchment paper. Set aside.

2. **Make the dough.** In a medium bowl, whisk the flour, baking soda, and salt to combine. Cut the butter into small cubes and add them to the flour mixture. Using your fingertips or a fork, mash the butter really well until the mixture resembles coarse sand. Stir in the raisins followed by the buttermilk, egg, and 2 tablespoons of sugar. Mix well until all the flour is moist and a stiff dough forms.

3. **Shape the dough.** As best you can, gather the dough and shape it into a large ball. Place the dough in the prepared Dutch oven. Using a sharp knife, score a large X into the surface. Sprinkle the remaining 2 tablespoons of sugar across the top of the dough.

4. **Bake.** Cover the pot and bake on the center rack for 30 minutes. Uncover and bake for 15 minutes more, until the bread is golden brown and sounds hollow when tapped.

5. **Cool and serve.** Let the bread cool in the Dutch oven for 15 minutes, then transfer to a cutting board and slice. Store at room temperature, wrapped in plastic wrap or aluminum foil, for up to 2 days, or slice and freeze for up to 1 month.

VARIATION TIP: Try currants instead of raisins, or spice up the loaf with ½ teaspoon of caraway seeds.

Caramelized Banana Bread

Serves 8 / **Prep time:** 20 minutes / **Cook time:** 1 hour 5 minutes

Using buttermilk, quick oats, pecans, and light brown sugar makes all the difference in this banana bread. But that's just the beginning. My secret tip is to roast the bananas (in their peels) to concentrate their sugars before mashing, resulting in a more intense banana flavor. For a quick and easy streusel topping, stir together 3 tablespoons quick oats, 3 tablespoons light brown sugar, 2 tablespoons coconut oil, and a pinch of salt. Sprinkle the streusel over the batter, then bake.

3 very ripe bananas in their peels

¼ cup refined coconut oil, plus more for preparing the Dutch oven

¾ cup buttermilk

½ cup quick cooking oats

1½ cups whole-wheat flour

¼ cup chopped pecans

1½ teaspoons baking powder

½ teaspoon salt

½ teaspoon ground cinnamon

¾ cup packed light brown sugar

1½ teaspoons vanilla extract

2 large eggs

1. **Preheat the oven.** Preheat the oven to 350°F. While the oven preheats, bake the bananas in their peels on a baking sheet for about 10 minutes, until the peels turn black. Coat a Dutch oven with coconut oil. Set aside.

2. **Hydrate the oats.** In a medium bowl, stir together the buttermilk and oats. Set aside.

3. **Combine the dry ingredients.** In a medium bowl, whisk the flour, pecans, baking powder, salt, and cinnamon until well mixed

4. **Mix the wet and dry ingredients.** Peel the bananas, place them in a small bowl, and mash with a fork. Measure 1⅓ cups of mashed banana and add it to the buttermilk mixture. Add the brown sugar, coconut oil, vanilla, and eggs. Stir well. Fold in the flour mixture and mix just until no lumps remain.

5. **Bake the bread.** Pour the batter into the prepared Dutch oven. Bake, uncovered, for 55 minutes. Let the bread cool in the Dutch oven for 15 minutes. Serve slices warm or cool. Refrigerate leftovers for up to 4 days.

Deep-Dish Pizza

Serves 4 / **Prep time:** 15 minutes, plus 45 minutes to rise / **Cook time:** 40 minutes

Need. Pizza. Now. We've all been there. Luckily, this deep-dish pizza is practically foolproof when you bake it on parchment paper in the Dutch oven. To help you get the most out of your pizza dough, knead it well and allow time for the dough to double in size. This recipe will fit in one large 7-quart Dutch oven or two small- to moderate-size Dutch ovens. The dough may be refrigerated for up to 16 hours or frozen in a sealed bag for up to 1 month.

1 cup lukewarm water

2½ teaspoons active
dry yeast

1 tablespoon honey

1 tablespoon olive oil, plus
more for preparing the
Dutch oven

2½ cups all-purpose flour,
plus more for dusting

1 teaspoon salt

¾ cup pizza sauce

2 cups shredded
mozzarella cheese

1. **Make the pizza dough.** In a medium bowl, stir together the warm water, yeast, and honey. Let the mixture sit for about 5 minutes, until it begins to foam, an indication that the yeast is active. Stir in the olive oil, 2 cups of flour, and the salt. Dust a work surface with the remaining ½ cup of flour and turn the dough out onto the prepared surface. Knead the dough for about 5 minutes, gradually working in the additional flour until the dough is smooth and only slightly sticky.

2. **Let the dough rise.** Coat the inside of a Dutch oven with olive oil. Place the dough in the prepared Dutch oven, turning it to coat with the oil. Cover the pot with the lid and let the dough rise in a warm place for about 30 minutes, until doubled in size. Remove the dough and knead for 1 minute. Return it to the Dutch oven, cover, and let the dough rise for about 15 minutes more, until doubled in size.

3. **Preheat the oven.** Preheat the oven to 425°F.

4. **Bake the pizza.** Halve the dough. Wrap half of the dough in plastic wrap and refrigerate it. Line a Dutch oven with parchment paper and put the remaining dough on top. Press down to form a flat, even layer. Bake for 15 minutes. Spread the pizza sauce over the dough and sprinkle with the cheese. Bake for about 22 minutes more, until the pizza is fully cooked. The outer crust should feel hard and have a hollow sound when tapped. Let rest for 5 minutes, then grab the parchment and lift up the pizza to remove it. Using a pizza wheel, cut the pizza into slices and serve.

TECHNICAL TIP: Add your favorite toppings when you add the cheese—just be sure to spread them out so everything has plenty of room to cook; this is especially true for high-moisture vegetables, such as mushrooms. This recipe was tested with sauce, 1 layer of cheese, and 1 topping. If you add lots of toppings, increase the bake time, up to 7 minutes longer, to account for added moisture.

RED WINE–POACHED PEARS, page *154*

Desserts

Dessert doesn't need to be a complicated affair. Not only can Dutch oven desserts be showstoppers, but they can also be made without a bunch of specialty tools. Puddings, cobblers, and cakes can all be adapted into scoopable versions ideal for the Dutch oven. As you'll see, you can achieve some delicious caramelization around the edges and along the bottom of a baked good with the Dutch oven, while the middle tends to stay ooey and gooey. Therefore, I like to play to the strengths of the Dutch oven and make things such as the Giant Chocolate Chip Cookie (page 163) and Brownie Pudding (page 159). You'll also run far less risk of desserts drying out and/or overflowing thanks to the Dutch oven's height, which you know is a big stress reliever if you've ever made cobbler.

For those times when you really don't want to turn on the oven, there are even no-bake desserts such as Cardamom Applesauce with Vanilla Ice Cream (page 155) and layer-and-chill Tiramisu (page 166). These desserts run the gamut from just sweet enough to rich indulgence, so there's something for everyone.

Mango Sticky Rice

Serves 6 / **Prep time:** 10 minutes, plus 3 hours to soak the rice / **Cook time:** 40 minutes

Traditionally, glutinous rice would be covered and steamed in a woven wooden basket set over a pot of boiling water. I actually bought one of those baskets in Thailand and carried it all over the country for a month just so I could make this dish at home. However, I've found that if you don't have the steamer basket, a sieve works just as well.

1½ cups sushi rice

1 (14-ounce) can full-fat
   coconut milk

⅓ cup sugar

¼ teaspoon salt

2 mangos

1 tablespoon toasted
   sesame seeds

1. **Rinse the rice.** Pour the rice into a fine-mesh sieve and set it over a medium bowl. Fill the bowl with water and slosh the rice around with your hand for several minutes. Let sit for 3 hours, then drain.

2. **Steam the rice.** Set the sieve with the rice over a Dutch oven of simmering water. Cover the pot and steam the rice for 30 to 40 minutes, until tender. Check the water level in the pot occasionally and add more if it gets low. Transfer the cooked rice to a bowl and cover with a plate.

3. **Make the coconut milk sauce.** While the rice cools, in a small saucepan over medium-high heat, combine the coconut milk, sugar, and salt. Cook, stirring occasionally, for 1 minute. Turn off the heat and leave to thicken while you cut the mangos.

4. **Cut the mangos and serve.** Peel the mangos. Cut on either side of the pit, which is in the middle, then thinly slice the flesh. To serve, scoop and press the rice into a measuring cup to mold. Turn it onto a serving plate and drizzle the coconut milk sauce over the rice. Fan the mango slices on top and sprinkle with toasted sesame seeds. Refrigerate leftovers for up to 2 days.

INGREDIENT TIP: Look for mangos that are both ripe and firm, because they hold their shape better when slicing.

Red Wine– Poached Pears

Serves 6 / **Prep time:** 5 minutes / **Cook time:** 30 minutes

Bosc pears are firmer than other pear varieties, making them ideal for poaching in liquid. Look for firm-yet-ripe pears that yield slightly when you press the end opposite the stem. Perfectly ripe pears need little more than a slow simmer in wine with spices. Despite their simplicity, these pears look incredibly gourmet served in a shallow bowl surrounded by the burgundy sauce.

3 Bosc pears

2 cups red wine, such as Cabernet or Merlot

1 teaspoon vanilla extract

2 teaspoons sugar

2 star anise pods (optional)

1. **Prepare the pears.** Peel the pears and halve them lengthwise. Remove the seeds and core. Set the pear halves in the Dutch oven and pour the red wine on top. Add the vanilla, sugar, and star anise (if using).

2. **Poach.** Bring the wine to a low simmer over medium heat. Cover the pot, leaving the lid slightly ajar. Cook for 8 minutes, checking frequently to ensure the liquid is bubbling only slightly. Flip the pears and cook for about 8 minutes more, until a skewer pierces the pear flesh very easily. Transfer the pears to shallow serving bowls.

3. **Reduce the wine.** With the lid off, bring the liquid to boil. Cook for about 15 minutes, just until the sauce thickens enough to coat the back of a spoon. Drizzle a large spoonful of sauce over each pear and serve. Refrigerate leftovers with the sauce for up to 3 days.

INGREDIENT TIP: For this recipe, choose a wine that is somewhere between dry and sweet, such as Cabernet Sauvignon. Although you could try a sweet wine like port, I recommend leaving the added sugar out because the sweetness intensifies as the sauce reduces.

Cardamom Applesauce with Vanilla Ice Cream

Serves 6 / **Prep time:** 20 minutes / **Cook time:** 30 minutes

As a kid, it never even occurred to me that a person could make applesauce. It was just "one of those things that comes from the store." Then, one day, my dad did exactly that because I was sick and he wanted to make me feel better. I watched in awe as he poured apple chunks into a big pot, and I inhaled what smelled like apple pie. I'll never forget how incredibly fresh tasting that homemade applesauce was, and I'm reminded of its magic anytime I make applesauce for someone I love.

Grated zest and juice
   of 1 lemon
2 pounds Granny
   Smith apples
2 pounds sweet red
   apples, such as Gala
⅓ cup packed light
   brown sugar
3 tablespoons
   unsalted butter
1½ teaspoons
   ground cardamom
¼ teaspoon salt
Vanilla ice cream,
   for serving

1. **Prepare the apples.** In a Dutch oven, combine the lemon zest and lemon juice. Peel, core, and roughly chop the apples. Add the apples to the pot, stirring to coat them in the lemon juice, which will help prevent them from turning brown.

2. **Cook the apples.** Turn the heat to medium-low. Stir in the brown sugar, butter, cardamom, and salt. Cover the pot and simmer for about 30 minutes, until the apples release their juices and become very tender. Using a wooden spatula, stir vigorously, breaking up larger pieces. Serve warm with a scoop of vanilla ice cream on top. Refrigerate leftovers in the Dutch oven for up to 5 days.

MAKE IT CLASSIC: Instead of cardamom, use 1 teaspoon of ground cinnamon.

Cookies and Cream Ice Cream Cake

Serves 8 / **Prep time:** 30 minutes, plus 11 hours to freeze

This creamy, crunchy ice cream cake is the perfect way to chill out on a hot summer afternoon—and there's no cooking involved! The hardest part is making room in the freezer and waiting for those vanilla and chocolate cookie layers to freeze.

1 gallon cookies and cream ice cream

1 (19-ounce) package chocolate sandwich cookies

4 tablespoons (½ stick) unsalted butter, melted

1 (16-ounce) jar fudge topping

1 (8-ounce) container frozen whipped topping, thawed

1. **Soften the ice cream.** Set the ice cream on the counter for 30 minutes to soften.

2. **Chop the cookies and make the crust.** You need about 36 sandwich cookies for this recipe. Using a chef's knife, chop the sandwich cookies well. Reserve 1 cup of the chopped cookies for topping the cake; put the remaining cookies in a Dutch oven with the melted butter. Stir to combine, then press down to form a crust.

3. **Layer the cake.** Using a spatula, spread the softened ice cream over the cookie crust. Cover the pot and freeze for 2 hours. Pour the fudge sauce over the ice cream layer and freeze for 1 hour more. Spread the whipped topping over the fudge layer and top with the reserved chopped cookies. Freeze overnight or for at least 8 hours.

4. **Serve.** Remove the Dutch oven from the freezer at least 20 minutes before serving. Once the cake has thawed slightly, use a spatula to slice it and serve. Tightly wrapped to prevent freezer burn, the ice cream cake can be frozen for up to 1 month. Thaw on the counter for 20 minutes for easy slicing.

Buttermilk Cherry Clafoutis

Serves 6 / Prep time: 15 minutes / Cook time: 35 minutes

I like the way "clafoutis" (cluh-foo-tee) rolls off the tongue, a charming word for this rustic French dessert. Plump sweet cherries push their way through a golden, crackly custard cake. It's such a simple dessert—fresh berries elevate it and buttermilk balances the sweetness with its welcome tang.

Unsalted butter, for
preparing the Dutch oven

1 pound sweet
black cherries

4 large eggs

½ cup granulated sugar

¼ cup packed light
brown sugar

1 cup buttermilk

2 teaspoons vanilla extract

¼ teaspoon salt

¾ cup all-purpose flour

Powdered sugar,
for dusting

Vanilla ice cream, for
serving (optional)

1. **Preheat the oven and prepare the Dutch oven.** Preheat the oven to 375°F. Coat the Dutch oven with butter.

2. **Prepare the cherries.** Stem and pit the cherries, then place them in the Dutch oven.

3. **Whisk the other ingredients.** In a medium bowl, whisk the eggs, granulated sugar, brown sugar, buttermilk, vanilla, salt, and flour until smooth. Pour the filling over the cherries.

4. **Bake and serve.** Bake for 10 minutes. Lower the oven temperature to 350°F and bake for about 25 minutes more, until the top swells and is springy to the touch. Dust with powdered sugar and serve warm with vanilla ice cream (if using). Cover and refrigerate leftovers for up to 3 days.

TECHNICAL TIP: If clumps form in the batter, strain it through a fine-mesh sieve over a bowl to break up any clumps.

INGREDIENT TIP: Make your own buttermilk by combining 1 cup of milk with 1 tablespoon of vinegar or freshly squeezed lemon juice. Let the mixture curdle for 2 minutes, then remove 1 tablespoon of the liquid. Proceed with the recipe.

Coconut Tapioca Pudding

Serves 6 / **Prep time:** 5 minutes, plus 30 minutes to hydrate the tapioca / **Cook time:** 15 minutes, plus 2 hours to chill

This cold pudding gets extra thick and creamy as it chills. To really show off the tapioca pearls, I like to serve the pudding in parfait glasses with a bit of toasted coconut or a dash of nutmeg on top. Small pearl tapioca is widely available and works perfectly well, but I sometimes order large tapioca pearls online for a more substantial mouthfeel.

1½ cups whole milk

1 (14-ounce) can full-fat
   coconut milk

Pinch salt

½ cup small pearl tapioca,
   or large pearl tapioca

¼ cup sugar

1 large egg yolk

Dried coconut flakes,
   for garnish

1. **Hydrate the tapioca pearls.** In a Dutch oven, stir together the milk, coconut milk, salt, and tapioca pearls. Let sit to hydrate for 30 minutes.

2. **Cook the tapioca pudding.** Add the sugar to the tapioca mixture and bring to a boil over medium-high heat. Immediately reduce the heat to medium-low to maintain a low simmer. Cook for 7 minutes, stirring often to prevent sticking, until the tapioca is soft and fully cooked.

3. **Add the egg yolk.** Turn off the heat and let the pudding cool for about 5 minutes. Whisk in the egg yolk until well combined.

4. **Chill to thicken.** Transfer the pudding to small serving dishes. Cover each with plastic wrap (aluminum foil will not create a tight enough seal to prevent a "skin" from forming), pressing it onto the surface of the pudding, and refrigerate for at least 2 hours or until the pudding is thick and set.

5. **Toast the coconut flakes and serve.** In a medium skillet over medium heat, toast the coconut flakes for about 4 minutes, stirring frequently, until golden. Sprinkle over the tapioca puddings to serve. Refrigerate leftovers for up to 4 days.

Brownie Pudding

Serves 8 / **Prep time:** 10 minutes / **Cook time:** 1 hour 5 minutes

This intense dessert is a cross between a brownie and a pudding, with a crackly top and soft, fudgy base. To achieve this effect, you bake the dessert in a Dutch oven set in a water bath. Coffee really heightens the flavor of chocolate, so I like to serve this warm with a scoop of coffee ice cream.

1 cup (2 sticks) cold
   unsalted butter
¼ cup semisweet
   chocolate chips
¾ cup cocoa powder
½ cup all-purpose flour
½ teaspoon salt
4 large eggs
2 cups sugar
2 teaspoons vanilla extract
Coffee ice cream,
   for serving

1. **Preheat the oven.** Preheat the oven to 325°F.

2. **Melt the butter.** In a Dutch oven over low heat, combine the butter and chocolate chips. Heat for about 5 minutes, just until melted, then turn off the heat. Set the Dutch oven inside a 12-by-15-inch baking pan (large enough to fit the Dutch oven and hold 2 inches of water).

3. **Mix the dry ingredients.** In a medium bowl, whisk the cocoa powder, flour, and salt. Set aside.

4. **Mix the wet ingredients.** In another medium bowl, whisk the eggs, sugar, and vanilla until very smooth, thick, and light yellow. Pour the egg mixture into the cooled Dutch oven and stir to combine with the melted chocolate. Add the flour mixture and stir again just until combined.

5. **Bake.** Place the baking pan with the Dutch oven in it on the center oven rack. Add just enough of the hottest tap water to the baking pan to come 2 inches up the sides of the Dutch oven. Bake for 1 hour. You want the edges of the pudding to be slightly firmer than the center, which should appear undercooked. Transfer the Dutch oven to a cooling rack for 15 minutes, then serve warm with coffee ice cream. Refrigerate leftovers for up to 4 days.

Vanilla-Rum Bread Pudding with Poppy Seeds

Serves 8 / **Prep time:** 15 minutes, plus overnight to soak /
Cook time: 2 hours, plus overnight to cool

You won't believe how good this bread pudding is. It's like a cross between custard and cake. The cream-saturated bread sits deeper in the Dutch oven than it would in a shallow baking pan, so you really need to soak the bread cubes overnight so the center doesn't collapse. This is definitely one of those desserts that tastes better after being chilled overnight and reheated. Poppy seeds are usually with the other spices; you can leave them out if you can't find them.

1 day-old French baguette

8 tablespoons (1 stick) unsalted butter, melted

½ vanilla bean, split, seeds scraped, pod discarded

3 tablespoons spiced rum

5 large eggs

1¾ cups sugar

¼ teaspoon salt

4 teaspoons poppy seeds

4 cups half-and-half

1. **Preheat the oven.** Preheat the oven to 325°F.

2. **Make the bread pudding.** Remove any hard crust from the ends of the baguette, then cut the bread into ½-inch-thick cubes. Put the bread in a Dutch oven and pour the melted butter over the top. In a large bowl, whisk the vanilla bean seeds and rum to break up the clumps of seeds. Add the eggs, sugar, and salt and whisk well to combine. Stir in the poppy seeds and half-and-half, then pour the mixture over the bread. Press down lightly so all the bread soaks up the custard. Cover and refrigerate overnight, or for at least 3 hours to allow the bread to absorb the liquid.

3. **Bake.** Bake, uncovered, for about 2 hours or until the top and edges are very brown. The center will appear tall and puffy right out of the oven but will settle a bit as it cools. Let cool, then refrigerate overnight so the custard-like base has time to set completely. To serve, reheat each slice in a 375°F oven for about 10 minutes, until just warmed through. Refrigerate leftovers for up to 5 days.

Strawberry Rhubarb Crumble

Serves 6 / **Prep time:** 15 minutes / **Cook time:** 50 minutes

Every spring, I pounce on the opportunity to buy fresh rhubarb with little more than a whim of tossing them with strawberries, sugar, and cornstarch. This sweet and sour combination melds beautifully under a buttery crumble and practically begs to be served with vanilla ice cream.

6 rhubarb stalks, sliced

8 ounces strawberries, stemmed and halved

½ cup granulated sugar

5 teaspoons cornstarch

2 teaspoons vanilla extract

½ teaspoon salt, divided

¾ cup all-purpose flour

6 tablespoons (¾ stick) unsalted butter, cubed

1 cup old-fashioned rolled oats

½ cup packed light brown sugar

1. **Preheat the oven.** Preheat the oven to 360°F.

2. **Mix the filling.** In a Dutch oven, stir together the rhubarb, strawberries, granulated sugar, cornstarch, vanilla, and ¼ teaspoon of salt, stirring and tossing the fruit until it's coated well. Set aside.

3. **Mix the topping.** In a medium bowl, whisk the flour and the remaining ¼ teaspoon of salt to combine. Add the butter. Using a fork, smash and work the butter into the flour until the butter pieces are no larger than peas. Stir in the oats and brown sugar, using your hands to squeeze some of the crumble mixture together to form some larger clumps for texture. Spread the crumble over the fruit.

4. **Bake.** Bake for 40 to 50 minutes, until the top is golden brown and the fruit is bubbling. Let cool for 10 minutes, then serve. Refrigerate leftovers for up to 4 days.

MAKE IT CONTEMPORARY: Spice things up: by adding ½ teaspoon of ground ginger to the filling and a pinch of ground cardamom or ½ cup of chopped pecans to the crumble topping.

Peach Cobbler

Serves 8 / **Prep time:** 20 minutes / **Cook time:** 40 minutes

When you walk by peaches and can smell them from several feet away, that's the peak moment to make peach cobbler. Of course, you can make this recipe before peaches are perfectly ripe, adding more sugar to make up for the fruit's underripeness, but I prefer to wait until the fruit is plump, sweet, and full of juicy goodness. I use organic or local no-spray peaches whenever I can for quality and flavor. By the way, peach cobbler and ice cream are thick as thieves, dontchaknow.

9 tablespoons (1 stick plus 1 tablespoon) unsalted butter, divided

1½ cups pastry flour

½ teaspoon salt

⅓ cup ice water

¼ cup sugar

1 teaspoon vanilla extract

14 fresh, ripe peaches, quartered and pitted

1. **Preheat the oven.** Preheat the oven to 375°F.

2. **Make the crumble.** Cut 8 tablespoons of butter into small cubes and put them in a medium bowl. Sift the flour and salt over the butter. Using 2 forks or a pastry cutter, mash the butter into the flour. You want the mixture to resemble wet sand. When no large clumps of butter remain, add the ice water, one tablespoon at a time, just until the dough sticks together. Gather the dough into a ball, without kneading, and refrigerate while you work on the filling.

3. **Make the filling.** In a Dutch oven over medium heat, melt the remaining 1 tablespoon of butter. Stir in the sugar and vanilla to combine, then turn off the heat and add the peaches. Toss well to coat.

4. **Assemble and bake.** Using your fingers, break the dough into crumbles—there's no need for perfection here—and sprinkle a thick layer of pastry crumbles over the peaches. Bake for about 40 minutes, until bubbly. Using a large spoon, scoop the cobbler into serving bowls. Serve warm with a scoop of vanilla ice cream, if desired. Refrigerate leftovers for up to 3 days.

Giant Chocolate Chip Cookie

 ONE POT

Serves 8 / **Prep time:** 10 minutes / **Cook time:** 35 minutes

Bigger is better—that's the axiom at work in this jumbo chocolate chip cookie. This pizookie ("pizza" + "cookie") simply must be experienced warm. You know the texture—soft, ooey-gooey, with chocolate puddles—it's the kind of richness you'll want to wash down with cold milk or vanilla ice cream. Speaking of rich, I've included both white and brown sugars to get just the right amount of chew and caramel flavor.

1 cup (2 sticks)
   unsalted butter

1 cup packed light
   brown sugar

½ cup granulated sugar

1 teaspoon vanilla extract

2 large eggs

2 cups plus 2 tablespoons
   all-purpose flour

1 teaspoon baking soda

½ teaspoon salt

1½ cups semisweet
   chocolate chips

1. **Preheat the oven.** Preheat the oven to 325°F.

2. **Melt the butter.** In a Dutch oven over medium heat, melt the butter. Add the brown sugar and granulated sugar. Turn off the heat and stir well until smooth. Let cool completely. Stir in the vanilla and eggs until well mixed.

3. **Mix the dry ingredients.** Stir in the flour, baking soda, and salt. Fold in the chocolate chips, then press the dough down into the bottom of the Dutch oven to form a flat layer.

4. **Bake.** Bake for 28 to 35 minutes, until the edges are golden brown, more or less, depending on whether you want the center to be really soft or firmer. Transfer the Dutch oven to a wire rack to cool for 5 minutes, then serve the cookie warm. Refrigerate leftovers for up to 4 days.

VARIATION TIP: Mix things up with a combination of semisweet chocolate chips and milk chocolate chunks, butterscotch chips, or white chocolate chips; just make sure you end up with 1½ cups total.

Fluffy Cheesecake

Serves 8 / **Prep time:** 20 minutes / **Cook time:** 55 minutes

Although this recipe is totally easy, it may be a departure from other cheesecakes you have made. Folding fluffy meringue into the cream cheese batter creates a cheesecake that bakes up light and puffy with a custard-like jiggle. Temperature plays an important role here, which is why the Dutch oven sits in a hot water bath as it bakes.

1 cup cream cheese

4 tablespoons (½ stick) unsalted butter

7 tablespoons whole milk

2 teaspoons vanilla extract

1½ tablespoons freshly squeezed lemon juice

6 large eggs, separated

¾ cup sugar, divided

¾ cup cake flour

2½ tablespoons cornstarch

¼ teaspoon salt

1. **Preheat the oven and prepare the Dutch oven.** Preheat the oven to 410°F. Set a Dutch oven inside a 12-by-15-inch baking pan (large enough to fit the Dutch oven and hold 2 inches of water).

2. **Melt the cream cheese.** In a medium microwave-safe bowl, combine the cream cheese, butter, and milk. Microwave for about 1 minute on high power, just until soft and partly melted. Whisk to remove any lumps. Whisk in the vanilla, lemon juice, egg yolks, and ¼ cup plus 2 tablespoons of sugar until smooth.

3. **Sift the flour.** Set a fine-mesh sieve over the cream cheese mixture and sift the cake flour, cornstarch, and salt into it. Whisk and set aside.

4. **Beat the egg whites until stiff peaks form.** In the bowl of a stand mixer fitted with the whisk attachment, or in a large bowl using a hand-held electric mixer, whip the egg whites on medium-high speed until foamy. Gradually add the remaining ¼ cup plus 2 tablespoons of sugar while beating. Beat for about 3 minutes, until the egg whites are fluffy, have a nice shimmer, and form stiff peaks (see tip). Gradually fold the egg white foam into the cream cheese mixture until combined.

5. **Bake the cheesecake inside the water bath.**
Pour the cheesecake batter into the Dutch oven.
Place the baking pan with the Dutch oven in
it on the bottom oven rack. Add just enough of
the hottest tap water to the baking pan to come
2 inches up the sides of the Dutch oven. Bake
for 18 minutes. Reduce the oven temperature
to 325°F and bake for 12 minutes more. Turn
off the oven and open the door slightly. Let the
cheesecake sit in the warm oven for 25 minutes.
Remove and let cool completely before serving.
Refrigerate leftovers for up to 3 days.

TECHNICAL TIP: "Stiff peaks" is a term that describes
the state of a whipped mixture when it stands straight
up without falling over. This usually takes about
5 minutes of mixing.

Tiramisu

Serves 8 / **Prep time:** 30 minutes, plus 10 hours to chill

A Dutch oven is the perfect vessel for assembling the alternating layers of espresso-dipped ladyfingers and slightly sweetened cream in traditional tiramisu. This is a no-bake dessert that gets its classic light texture from aerating mascarpone and then letting everything settle into place in the refrigerator.

⅔ cup strong
  brewed espresso
3 tablespoons dark
  rum, divided
8 ounces
  mascarpone cheese
2 large eggs, separated
¼ cup sugar, divided
1 cup heavy
  (whipping) cream
¼ teaspoon vanilla extract
Pinch salt
20 ladyfinger cookies
Cocoa powder, for dusting

1. **Make the espresso.** In a small bowl, combine the espresso with 1 tablespoon of dark rum. Set aside to cool.

2. **Make the mascarpone cream.** In the bowl of a stand mixer fitted with the whisk attachment, or in a large bowl using a handheld electric mixer, beat the mascarpone and the remaining 2 tablespoons of rum on medium speed until smooth. Set aside.

   Place a medium heatproof bowl over a pot of shallow simmering water—you don't want the water to touch the bowl. In the bowl, whisk the egg yolks and 2 tablespoons of sugar for about 5 minutes, until light and foamy. Pour the egg yolk mixture over the mascarpone mixture and beat just until combined. Set aside.

   In another medium bowl, beat the heavy cream and vanilla on medium-high speed for about 4 minutes, just until medium peaks form—the whipped cream should appear soft and pillowy. Fold the whipped cream into the mascarpone mixture just until incorporated. Set aside.

In a clean, dry bowl of a stand mixer fitted with a clean whisk attachment, or a large bowl using a handheld electric mixer, beat the egg whites and salt on medium-high speed for about 2 minutes, until foamy. Add the remaining 2 tablespoons of sugar and beat for about 5 minutes more, until stiff peaks form. Fold the egg whites into the mascarpone mixture.

3. **Assemble the layers.** Set a Dutch oven on a work surface next to the ladyfingers, coffee mixture, and mascarpone mixture. Quickly dip each side of half of the ladyfingers, one at a time, into the espresso mixture and lay them flat in the Dutch oven to form the first layer. Place half the mascarpone mixture on top, spreading it evenly. Proceed to dip the remaining ladyfingers into the espresso mixture and form another layer on top of the mascarpone. Top with the remaining mascarpone mixture, spreading it evenly.

4. **Refrigerate.** Cover the pot and refrigerate for 2 hours. Sift cocoa powder over the top and refrigerate again for at least 8 hours, or up to 1 day. Using a large spoon, scoop the chilled tiramisu onto serving plates; you can dip the spoon into warm water to make serving each portion prettier. Refrigerate leftovers for up to 3 days.

SUBSTITUTION TIP: If you can't make espresso, use instant coffee instead. Mix 3 tablespoons of instant coffee with ⅔ cup of warm water.

MEASUREMENT CONVERSIONS

VOLUME EQUIVALENTS	U.S. STANDARD	U.S. STANDARD (OUNCES)	METRIC (APPROXIMATE)
LIQUID	2 tablespoons	1 fl. oz.	30 mL
	¼ cup	2 fl. oz.	60 mL
	½ cup	4 fl. oz.	120 mL
	1 cup	8 fl. oz.	240 mL
	1½ cups	12 fl. oz.	355 mL
	2 cups or 1 pint	16 fl. oz.	475 mL
	4 cups or 1 quart	32 fl. oz.	1 L
	1 gallon	128 fl. oz.	4 L
DRY	⅛ teaspoon		0.5 mL
	¼ teaspoon		1 mL
	½ teaspoon		2 mL
	¾ teaspoon		4 mL
	1 teaspoon		5 mL
	1 tablespoon		15 mL
	¼ cup		59 mL
	⅓ cup		79 mL
	½ cup		118 mL
	⅔ cup		156 mL
	¾ cup		177 mL
	1 cup		235 mL
	2 cups or 1 pint		475 mL
	3 cups		700 mL
	4 cups or 1 quart		1 L
	½ gallon		2 L
	1 gallon		4 L

OVEN TEMPERATURES

FAHRENHEIT	CELSIUS (APPROXIMATE)
250°F	120°C
300°F	150°C
325°F	165°C
350°F	180°C
375°F	190°C
400°F	200°C
425°F	220°C
450°F	230°C

WEIGHT EQUIVALENTS

U.S. STANDARD	METRIC (APPROXIMATE)
½ ounce	15 g
1 ounce	30 g
2 ounces	60 g
4 ounces	115 g
8 ounces	225 g
12 ounces	340 g
16 ounces or 1 pound	455 g

INDEX

ACKNOWLEDGMENTS

I am forever grateful to my publisher, Callisto Media; my editor, Britt Bogan; and *The Frayed Apron*'s readers for the opportunity to publish my first book. I would like to thank my darling husband for supporting my call to a creative life, reading my work, taste testing, and being my rock. Thank you to my mom for saving every book I ever made and encouraging my writing and cooking since the beginning of time. Thank you to my dad for your bread baking enthusiasm, which was no doubt a starting point for my own love of baking. Thank you to my uncle Eddie for your generosity and for spoiling me with Le Creuset Dutch ovens. Thank you to my family for taste testing my creations and for your helpful feedback. Thank you to the Natural Gourmet Institute for adopting me into the culinary world and nurturing my culinary voice.

ABOUT THE AUTHOR

Sara Furcini is a chef and creator of the food blog *The Frayed Apron*. She grew up in the Arizona desert and went to culinary school in New York City, where she went on to teach cooking classes and work in a Michelin star restaurant. Her culinary experiences and her travels drove Sara to food writing and photography as a way of sharing her passion with others. When she's not in the kitchen creating recipes, Sara likes to explore nature with her husband and dog.

Visit Sara at TheFrayedApron.com for tried-and-true recipes and cooking tips.

CPSIA information can be obtained
at www.ICGtesting.com
Printed in the USA
LVHW020302231021
701210LV00004B/4

9 781647 396978